*The Missionary Spirit
In Parish Life*

THE
MISSIONARY SPIRIT
IN PARISH LIFE

by

Abbé G. Michonneau ·

THE NEWMAN PRESS
Westminster, Maryland
1952

Nihil obstat: Edward A. Cerny, S.S., D.D.,
          Censor librorum.

Imprimatur: Most Reverend Francis P. Keough, D.D.,
            Archbishop of Baltimore.
November 19, 1951.

Preface

WHEN *Revolution in a City Parish* [1] WAS IN THE MAKING, one thought was a constant source of uneasiness to us. It was this: Could we trust our brother priests to take these "conclusions of five years' experience" for what they were, without trying to find in them what they were never meant to contain? Would our brother priests see that there was much more to them than a collection of recipes and ingenious devices to be used, adapting them as well as possible, to transform their parishes? Were we putting enough stress on the main thing, the thing we were really interested in—the priestly life, the missionary spirit? Without it, no method, no matter how good it is, will have any apostolic effectiveness; with it, no matter what the methods used, it is possible to succeed in doing God's work.

This uneasiness has continued to haunt us, to haunt us in direct ratio to the favor *Revolution in a City Parish* has met with. Our book broached many problems; it had to, since we were concerned with the whole question of a "parish policy." But now the time has come for us to set aside concern for both methods and experiences and go right to the heart of the problem, speaking to the priest and about the priest only. Such is the aim of this new book.

---

[1] This is the English title of the book *Paroisse, Communauté Missionnaire* (by the same authors: Fathers Michonneau and Chéry) to which frequent reference is made in the present work.

Contents

PREFACE   **v**

I   THE MISSIONARY PROBLEM IS PRIMARILY A
PRIESTLY PROBLEM   1

II   ON CERTAIN FORMS OF THE PSEUDO-MISSIONARY
SPIRIT   20

     The Ritualistic Spirit   22
     The Pioneering Spirit   27
     The Planning Spirit   29
     The Social-Worker Spirit   33
     The Proprietary Spirit   36
     The Competitive Spirit   38
     The Pseudo-Mystical Spirit   40
     The Pseudo-Angelic Spirit   41

III   ON THE NEED OF HAVING SOMETHING TO
REPLACE WHAT WE DESTROY   47

     Church Recreation Centers   50
     The Question of the Solemn Communion   53
     The Care of the Sick   57
     The Parish Milieu   58
     The Missionary Himself   61

IV   THE ESSENCE OF THE MISSIONARY SPIRIT   67

     Vision of the World   67
         A Man of Conviction   68
         A Realist   72
         An Uneasy Man   78

Contents

IV   THE ESSENCE OF THE MISSIONARY SPIRIT (*Cont.*):
     Vision of the World (*Cont.*):
     A Victim   83
     Vision of the Church   86
     Vision of the Love of Christ   100

V   SOME MATERIALS FOR A MISSIONARY SPIRITU-
     ALITY   105
     "Missionary"?   106
     Mortification Through the Ministry or
     Through Spiritual Exercises?   108
     Meditation   124
     Faith   129
     Hope   138
     Charity   149
     A Cardinal Missionary Virtue:
     Graciousness   155
     An Exercise to Add: The Sabbatical Rest   164

VI   THE ABSOLUTE NEED OF TEAMWORK   171
     The Theological Basis   173
     The Advantages for Us Priests   175
     Advantages for Missionary Work   187
     A Good School for Apprentices   191

*The Missionary Spirit
In Parish Life*

I

The Missionary Problem Is Primarily a Priestly Problem

What chance to succeed has the missionary effort now being undertaken in France? The more one reflects on this subject, the more convinced does one become that it is the caliber of the men undertaking it—or, more precisely, their value as priests—that will decide. This is an elementary truth, even a truism. And there has never been a seminary rector who has not been convinced of it. But it is one thing to come to such a theoretical conclusion, as you meditate on the four Gospels, the Epistle to the Hebrews, the tract on the priesthood, and the Pontifical's admirable monitions to the ordinands; and quite another thing to reach the same conclusion every day through listening, in grief or wonder, to lay people pour out the secrets of their hearts, or through seeing with your own eyes, in the parishes you visit, how the spread of the gospel is affected by the kind of priests you find in them. During his years of training, when as yet he knows but little of the outward conditions in

1

which he will have to practice the virtues that are preached to him, every normal seminarian has his mind occupied with this thought; but when a priest has seen the principle work out, it becomes an obsession with him.

Good priests, thank God, are legion in France. Pious, regular in their ministry, faithful to their duties, devoted to their parish activities, they certainly deserve the esteem generally accorded them. Why, then, is their influence so limited? Why do the parishes over which they preside appear lifeless, static, dormant, as is unfortunately so often the case? Could it be that the priestly virtues have, in view of the needs of our times, been imperfectly grasped or incorrectly reduced to practice?

Try asking Catholic Action leaders, or, without asking them, keep your ears open for what they have to say. Learn to pay attention to the remarks of those who do not go to church. There are some, of course, who have an ax to grind, and there is no need to bother with them; but the rest, what do they say? What do they look for and expect in a priest? Only the virtues a priest ought to have. What do they complain of? Only that we are not sufficiently priests! They have a very high and splendid ideal for us, but one which is truly the ideal of the priesthood. They do not expect us to be artists or scholars or administrators or businessmen or specialists. In the final analysis, they ask nothing from us that is foreign to our mission. Even the intellectuals do not expect us to dazzle them with our erudition or to be clever at juggling with theories. They ask us only to give them some solid food, because they want to avoid malnutrition if they can.

The laboring man will not necessarily give his trust to the priest who affects the ways of the working class. He will perhaps think the priest a good fellow; but unless he senses something more than that in him, it is not to that priest he will go when in real need of help, but to another, to one whom he feels to be a man of God. The case is no different with the professional man. He will be glad to invite to his table a "distinguished" priest, whose fine manners, polished conversation, and literary culture will charm his family and his guests; but when he runs into troubles of conscience or family difficulties, it is to a true priest that he will go for help, even though the true priest may lack all these attractive qualities.

We ourselves know of a parish in which the practicing Catholics are predominantly middle-class and in which the busiest confessional is that of the assistant who is least middle-class. The "bourgeois" complain of his sermons, saying that he is a demagogue. The more refined people smile at his clumsy language. And the young ladies of the parish often make fun of the some-what careless way he dresses. Yet at his confessional you see lines of young ladies and intellectuals and "bour-geois" as well as Jocists. When it comes to going to "the priest," people forget everything else.

What does everyone ask for? First of all: for apostolic priests, who do not look on visitors as a matter of indifference, much less as a bother; but rather as human beings, each of whom has a life all his own to live, and

3

as children of God, to each of whom the Father desires to show His love.

A young man has just died, killed in the Paris Resistance. His sister, who loved him dearly, has been brought up, like him, without religion. Yet in her distress she goes to visit a priest. She is not a totally unreligious person; on the contrary, she would like to hear something about that other world to which her brother has just gone. The priest gives her the titles of a few books—excellent ones, no doubt, for the purpose. But she goes away disillusioned, and will never come back. It is not a book she is looking for, but the living words of one who was touched by her suffering, the echo of Him who wept at the tomb of Lazarus.

A workingman comes to ask for baptism—a skilled worker, very good at his job, and not at all stupid. But he cannot read or write. How will he be able to learn "the catechism"? The priest sends him away. Does he hope the man will get down to study the alphabet and come back when he can make out "Who is God?"

Another man (one who knows how to read) comes to ask for instruction preliminary to baptism, and immediately the priest says to him, "Fine, my good man. I am going to turn you over to the Sister . . ." Later, it is true, this might be the normal thing—and yet . . . But at this first contact had the priest nothing more that he could say?

And then this other man, who is having a very hard time leading a Christian life and goes to confession in the hope of finding some help—what does he hear from

4

the confessor? Only the nice little ready-made sermon which did service for the pious lady before him and will do for the child after him as well; but he receives nothing personal, nothing to make him think that the confessor even grasped what he told him. And in the end, he grows tired of it, for he feels that he is all alone; it will be four years before he has recourse to the sacraments again, and then only when a lay friend of his brings him to a priest who is happy to "lose" an hour with him.

A pastor sees a man enter his confessional just after leaving the confessional of the first assistant, and this is what the man tells him: "Father, I have just been to confession to your assistant, and there is something I want to tell you. It is forty years since I have been to confession, and he had nothing to say to me."

If these were isolated cases, we would not even mention them, any more than we shall mention the few unfortunate priests who abandon their vocation. But the truth is that sad incidents such as these are happening every day. There is something missing. Call it the flaming zeal of an apostle or a kind of passion for souls; but whatever you call it, it is something that makes a man act and look and speak in a way that sets him apart from the mere conscientious official who does his assigned task efficiently. There is lacking that freshness of outlook which enables us to be just as much struck by every case that comes our way as we were on the first day, just as much moved by the last secret entrusted to us as we were by the first. Yet it is just such a fresh outlook that we need, because the last soul we will be called upon to assist in our ministry and the last individual whose spiritual anguish is laid bare to us will be just as important as the first. To the man who comes to see us it makes no difference that others like him have preceded him. To him his case, his grief, his disquiet, his joy are altogether new and full of interest.

At a meeting held in England for the purpose of study and exchange of views, we recently had the opportunity to listen to laymen from twelve different countries express their opinions. On one point they all agreed: "We lack priests able to understand us and help us." And it was possible to read between the lines and glimpse a situation far more painful than their words expressed.

Our laymen also ask for priests who have eyes to see not only the real problems that exist in the parish but also those that concern the nation and the world. It is not, of course, revolutionaries or agitators that they want, but priests unshackled by routine, priests who will make the effort to discover the real work that has to be undertaken over and above what has always been done. The laity of whom we are here speaking are obviously those individuals who are deeply concerned for the spread of the gospel—not the old guard, whose one worry is fear of change, whether it be the time of the Mass or their seat in church. The former, whose concern for the spread of the gospel is so laudable, may well be scandalized when they hear a priest exclaim, "We've had enough reforms; give us some rest!" Péguy would answer, "The saints were not men of rest." The new forms of charity which St. Vincent de Paul was incessantly inventing disturbed the rest of a great many people, and very often officials must have said to him, "That's enough; give us a chance to breathe!" St. Vincent, however, with his even pace, which never outstripped Providence, continued to advance steadily; and every morning he looked on human misery with fresh eyes and tirelessly kept on creating new remedies for it. It is men like that who extend the kingdom of God, men who know that "new wine is not to be put in old wineskins," men who have not come to terms with things as they are.

Such an attitude calls for courage: not merely the courage required to emerge from ourselves and our way of doing things, or the courage to remake ourselves continually without becoming attached to what we have loved and accomplished; but also the courage to show others the way, to win others over and rouse them to action, to transform them into apostles, to bring them to accept—or better still, to discover for themselves—the new roads that have to be travelled. People expect us not to be timid. How many men of good will there are who, sometimes even without knowing it, would be eager to volunteer if they were only called upon! And how much bad will would melt away like snow in the sun if only the sun were hot enough—that is, if only the priest were an enthusiastic optimist radiating conviction and an infectious confidence in his cause!

The priest is expected to be filled with the charity of the gospel, the charity which St. Paul says "spurs us on," and to which alone we can look to produce the qualities

7

just mentioned: the missionary spirit, zeal for souls, the anxious desire to do better, the daring of the saints. People want to feel that the charity of Christ is in the heart of the priest; and they want the priest's words, both public and private, to be an expression of his love. The main thing is, not that we should be good publicity men, alert to every opportunity, but that we should be men with hearts on fire, men in whom the Spirit of Pentecost continues to live on. That is why the people expect us to be one heart and one soul, as the first Apostles were. They look for us to be priests who love one another and understand one another, who live a community life, who carry on their apostolic work as one man.

Besides, when we take the trouble to investigate thoroughly the reasons why the Christian spirit has, in certain environments and regions, proved incapable of resisting decline or corruption, it becomes evident that in most cases the unhappy state must be traced to priests who were not up to the mark. Why, for example, do the great number of Catholics who come from a solidly Catholic region of our country abandon the practice of religion as soon as they arrive in Paris? The reason is that their priests failed to give them a true Christian formation. Why do such people often prove more anticlerical than others? Because, before coming to Paris, they had had the experience, in those Catholic regions, of a clericalism that proved oppressive.

A few examples might be welcome. A young priest has just sung his first Mass in his home parish. To celebrate the event, his boyhood friends have prepared a feast in his honor in the village square. The young priest, who has dined at the rectory and is uneasy at the thought that his friends have been kept waiting for him, asks the pastor for permission to leave. "My dear boy," answers the pastor, "now that you are a priest, you will have to learn to make people wait for you."

Passing by a church, a man from another parish decides to go to Mass there. On the bulletin board of the church he reads that Mass is at seven o'clock and, as it is already ten minutes after seven and there is no one at the altar, he rings the rectory doorbell. "Is there going to be a Mass today, Father? It is after seven and I don't see anyone." "My good man," replies the pastor from the window as he buttons his cassock, "it will be seven when I get there."

And anticlericalism is perhaps not the worst fruit of such bad principles and attitudes, for they have also produced formalism. If so many Catholics no longer have a genuine Christian mentality, may not the reason be that they were often expected to conform outwardly when they had received no interior formation? External actions and practices were demanded of them, and they were required to use formulas; yet no one gave them the ideas and convictions which originally gave birth to the formulas. External deportment was so stressed that it acquired the status of a virtue. Only recently, in a certain parish young girls were refused absolution for having taken to wearing hats instead of *coiffes* and for riding bicycles. We admit children to baptism without

9

having had any conversation with their parents, without saying a single word to them; instead, we hurry as fast as we can through a sorry ceremony at the back of the church. When engaged couples come to arrange for a marriage, all we do is ask them how expensive a wedding they want and write down their answers to the pre-nuptial questionnaire (which, by the way, could provide us with an excellent missionary opening); then we require the young man to make a sacramental confession that will be a farce. We water down Christian obligations by agreeing to all sorts of compromises and concessions. Our demands are exacting only when it is a question of externals. And yet when the externals are those of our own priestly functions (celebration of Mass and administration of the sacraments), the faithful who attend see us show so very little reverence! Unless they have a very deep faith, how can they fail to conclude that all this is a sham and that religion has no real basis at all? What other explanation is there for such a state of affairs but that the faith of priests is not strong enough to be infectious and their life not interior enough to make them emphasize chiefly the things of the interior? "We have too many administrators," Cardinal Suhard used to sigh, "too many administrators and not enough priests."

The main task, therefore, the one that has priority over all others, is the making of good priests. When we say this, we are not for a moment forgetting the indispensable role which belongs to laymen in the work of spreading the gospel. But the two problems are closely connected; and the problem of the formation of priests must obviously take precedence, for the priesthood of the laity will never have a chance to be exercised if the priesthood of the priests is not strong enough to give the other the impetus it must have. To form true priests and then to keep them up to the mark, to develop them and to make the fullest use of them—these are the principal tasks that confront us in our day.

What we ask of seminaries is this: a training devised and carried through with the idea of giving to Catholics —and non-Catholics—the apostles they need, not individualists accustomed to thinking and praying and working in isolation, but teammates animated by the need of holding together and exerting influence as leaders. It is priests with really priestly souls that are called for, priests so conscious of the demands of the missionary ideal, priests so eager to do all they can, that they will never be likely to use a canon of the Code as an excuse for taking it easy.

When the young priest, just out of the seminary, is beginning his life in the ministry, with what care should he not be surrounded, if he is to keep and develop the apostolic fire indispensable for fruitful missionary work! How sad it is to see him so often placed in situations that can rob him of all his life and all his enthusiasm! It is regrettable that there are still only a few dioceses where this problem can be easily dealt with. We all know too well how the shortage of priests and the difficulty of filling vacancies crowd all other considerations off the stage. But does this justify leaving young priests, at the beginning of their ministry, in an isolation that breeds depression? Does it justify transferring them ever more frequently (one of our confreres has been in three different places within two years), without giving them a chance to get a start at serious work? And does it justify placing young priests under a pastor who is discouraging, sour, dictatorial, or else so indifferent that his assistants feel that they cannot count on any support in the tasks that face them?

In one of our dioceses, plans had been made for the establishment of a missionary deanery. Three priests had formed a team for the enterprise. A friend of theirs was ready to join them and was to be assigned to a parish in the deanery. But at the last moment the pastor who was to make room for him by moving to another parish backed down on the agreement, and the young priest was named to a chaplaincy . . . Customs may, of course, be so strong as to make it practically impossible to transfer a priest against his will. But this at least must be clear: that, in the first place, the priest who stubbornly stands in the way lacks the real spirit of the priesthood; and that, in the second, such customs ought to be reconsidered, since they go against the common good.

We have already spoken about certain flaws which hinder the work of the apostolate. These flaws, it is worth pointing out, are to be blamed much less on the men involved than on the established customs. They are almost inevitable as long as we do not form communities of priests who will give each other mutual support and assistance, and as long as we do not place together men who can do good work together.

It is all very well to say that the young priest must keep his spirit, his sacred fire. But if the present system continues, if three or four parishes are committed to a single priest instead of a team being placed in the center of ten or twelve parishes, how can anyone expect this young man, isolated and without support, to keep his zeal for long, when he sees himself alone to confront the indifferent mass of people he is supposed to rouse?

It is all very well to say that the young priest must do intellectual work, that he must read and reflect on his ministry, that he must not slip into the rut of routine. But how is he to do all this without a stimulus? He is hardly likely to find what he needs at the deanery conferences, where from time to time he will meet pastors whose basic orientation (if indeed they have any) is quite different from his own. Often enough, he will find quite the contrary and will go back to his solitude less strong than before. He needs books and reviews which, in his poverty, he cannot obtain for himself, but which a team could obtain. He needs to be able to exchange views with priests engaged in the same kind of work. He needs the advice of an older man with whom he could do good work, finding in him both experienced counsel and needed companionship. In a community life we learn a great deal, since we are able to take lessons from one another by comparing our ideas and confronting our projects.

And from the spiritual viewpoint, is there any substitute for a common life in which men pray together and feel that they are brothers with the same apostolic interests? Is it not true that the Holy Spirit dwells in such communities?

Even on the material plane—as has been pointed out a hundred times but needs to be continually emphasized—it is quite obviously a crushing responsibility for a priest to have to look after so many things, which none the less he cannot eliminate. There is his food, its preparation, the business of fuel and heating, his own needs and those of the church to be provided for, including the needs of the parish activities—all those terrible money problems which dog his every step. The formation of communities will not, of course, do away with these; but it will lighten them, because the burdens will be divided and there will be several priests to put their shoulders to the task. In this way, too, it is possible to lessen the contrast between the so-called "good" parishes, where a living comes comparatively easy, and those where priests find it impossible to make ends meet.

Let us make no mistake about it: the power of priests to maintain their missionary spirit, once they have begun their ministry, depends to a very great extent on the way they are utilized, whether in isolation or in community.

It also depends on the degree of fatherly interest that they feel their superiors take in them. In some large dioceses, the administration spirit colors everything and takes precedence over everything else—even over the relationship which ought to exist between sons and fathers: between sons who can be free and open, and fathers whose benevolence is full of solicitude.

It is true that we must have administration; but let it be, as an old legal expression puts it, the administration of the father of a family. The priest ought to feel that he belongs to a family and that he is ruled by something more than decrees and statutes. *Dominus regit me et nihil mihi deerit . . . Virga tua et baculus ipsa me consolata sunt . . . et misericordia tua subsequetur me omnibus diebus vitae meae . . .*

With good reason all our dioceses are disturbed over the falling off in vocations to the priesthood. Yet religious communities today are attracting more vocations. What are we to conclude? That these young men (for generally it is not a question of boys, but of young, and sometimes even mature, men) are mistaken in thinking their vocation is to a religious community, whereas in reality it is to the diocesan clergy? Or that communities resort to excessive propagandizing and a method of recruiting that is out of order? Perhaps, in the case of one or the other modern community, such a reproach is justified. Perhaps even, now and then, there is a certain amount of self-deception in some individuals' infatuation for the religious life. But it would be a much more serious self-deception to concentrate on such cases and fail to see further into the matter. In fact, the root reason seems quite certainly to lie in the way the young view the life of the secular priest. What the young want, when they are about to give themselves, is to do so completely and thoroughly. They are looking for a priestly life which is one hundred per cent priestly. They take a look around and see the conditions in which many a secular priest is called upon to live. They notice how isolated he is; and, knowing that they themselves are not made of iron, they fear that they could not live like that for a lifetime. It is easy to call them cowards or deserters. Much too easy. We ourselves know many who realize quite well that it is the parish priest who is called upon to fight the most important battle. We know that they would prefer to enter directly into the great work of the diocesan clergy, that at times they have to do violence to themselves in order to embrace the religious life with all that it implies. But they embrace it nevertheless, because for them the development of their priesthood takes first place. When they give their life, their only fear is that some day they may take it back again.

Who would dare to blame them? What most attracts the young is the example of an apostolic priest living in the present—that, and the assurance that their priestly lives will not be wasted, that they will have a chance to be real priests, that they will be given the training they require and, when the time comes, will receive both the appointment that suits their ability and the support they need. They never bother to ask themselves whether they will depend on the Pope through the intermediary of a bishop or of a superior general. What interests them is, not whether the diocesan community is the sole priestly community of divine institution or not, but rather: *where* they will find a priestly community that is a reality. The drama enacted in their hearts is not one in which the terms "diocesan" and "non-diocesan" play the principal roles, and any attempt to make them look at the problem in this light is artificial and doomed to failure.

It is not much truer to say that some are looking for a particular form of the apostolate—say, preaching, teaching, or Catholic Action. They have their preferences, of course, and often enough these are for parish work. But, taking them all in all, they are expendable and will prove it later on by their docility to the direction of superiors. In point of fact, what they want above all else is the means of sanctification during and after their period of formation, the hope of teamwork, the warm and friendly atmosphere of a family. What they find most repugnant is the prospect of a priestly ministry degenerating into a merely perfunctory performance of official duties.

Let us once have a great many parishes where priests may live the communal life in its fullness; let us once see whole dioceses offer their future priests seminaries where they will be formed according to their spiritual needs and their life work; let us see dioceses offer their priests in the ministry the opportunity for apostolic and fraternal teamwork—then vocations to the diocesan clergy will once again be numerous. In a word: give them the possibility, the assurance that they will not be left alone but will be able to count on assistance all their life long, and you will not have to warn them against the seductions of the religious life. For many of them, the secular priesthood will be enough; but, to use a proverb, we

17

must not put the cart before the horse and ask the young to sacrifice their legitimate aspirations in order to further reforms which could be initiated today.

Besides, it is obvious that this work is already being undertaken in many places and that it has already attracted many vocations, as in the case of the Mission of Paris. It is in this direction we must work—a direction which we would like to call "the reassessment of the priestly vocation."

Revolution in a City Parish has occasioned our receiving the confidences of a great many lay people. Most of them, sad to say, struck the same note: "Oh, if our pastor would only . . ." "If our pastor only understood!" "If our pastor would only get into it!" The same plaintive cry seems to go up on all sides. Sometimes it took another form: "I have no one to go to. There are many priests in the city, but I cannot find a spiritual director." Of course, we must be wary in appraising such complaints. Yet it is also true that when we see the work there is to do, especially when we see how slow is the progress and how sometimes there is none, we cannot fail to reach the conclusion that it is the question of the priesthood that counts before everything else. Whether you discuss the problems of the apostolate with bishops or priests or laymen, with believers or unbelievers, with laboring or professional men, with intellectuals or with plain people, you always come back to the same point, the point with which you must start: "We need priests," they will all tell you, "many priests; but above all we need priests with the missionary spirit, priests working together shoulder to shoulder and in the charity of Christ."

One comes back from a trip abroad convinced that it is in France especially that there exists not only this desire but also the beginning of its fulfillment. We do not believe that anywhere else such an admirable effort is being made to produce a missionary clergy, both secular and regular. Our readers in neighboring lands need have no doubt about this: the longings we are expressing are those of the great majority of the French clergy, and every day they are being translated into realities and in a way that gives us every reason to hope for tomorrow.

Our desire is that this effort may not be compromised by excesses and deviations. To these we shall devote the next chapter.

II

On Certain Forms of the Pseudo-Missionary Spirit

"Accept no substitutes."

All valuable things, from bank notes to superior brands of candy and biscuits, have their imitations. It is the same in matters of religion. The four authentic Gospels were succeeded by a swarm of apocryphal gospels. For one apparition of the Virgin that has all the marks of genuineness and is acknowledged by the Church, twenty are produced by the imagination and the Church has to disown them. The magnificent Thomism of the thirteenth century degenerated into the hairsplitting scholasticism of the fourteenth, and is again found (not easily recognizable, though still bearing the name) six or seven hundred years later in certain manuals for seminary use. All our dogmas have had their counterfeits, which we call heresies. Every movement to renew the life of the Church—from the monastic movements to those of Catholic Action—has had its fanatics, its bigots, its dead weights, its eccentrics.

Ordinarily, loss of equilibrium is responsible for this phenomenon, emphasis being put on one aspect to the detriment of another, and generally on a secondary, external aspect to the detriment of the essence and of the spirit.

Corruptio optimi pessima. There is no sadder sight than the disintegration of something that was great and fine.

The missionary movement is not immune to this danger; but, if we are to protect ourselves against it, we must look it in the face, especially since the enemy is to be found not only in others. He is in every man and can be the ruin of anyone who is not on his guard.

In those whom we shall call "pseudo-missionaries" all the stock defects are to be found. There is the spirit of the Pharisee ("Thanks, Lord, that I am not like the rest of men . . ."); the spirit of rivalry and of criticism of those fellow workers of ours who will not adopt our pet ideas in their entirety; the spirit of independence towards authority; the spirit of taking the easy way (and therefore the spirit of laziness), which rests content with the slight effort required to apply recipes (the recipes being considered as cure-alls); the "nominalist" spirit, hypnotized by words; the superficial spirit, which would change everything except itself and which tends to take refuge from necessary tasks in dreaming. Every one of these is, of course, clothed with the finest "missionary" pretexts.

With the reader's permission we intend to caricature these in our own way. The originals of our caricatures doubtless do not exist in the pure state, but this attempt exposes tendencies which are in all of us and which all of us must check.

The man with the ritualistic spirit is very hard on the liturgical fanatics, whose horizon is limited to a network of rubrics. If you were to tell him that he is a rubricist without knowing it, he would be quite amazed. And still he too has his ritual—a ritual with its vestments, its magic words, its attitudes, its external actions.

What is the secret of being an apostle? It is really quite simple: you have only to wear a work shirt and a heavy belt, cultivate a military or a proletarian air, and take off the clerical garb, if necessary . . . Over a drink of wine, such an apostle calls a friend "Buddy," and thinks that he has won over every worker in the bar— who did not realize they were letting themselves in for this! . . . He makes his little mark as the priest of "the little people," quite proud of being ashamed of the bourgeois and never suspecting that the workers accept him only with a kind of sly amusement.

If he finds life in the parish boring or if he is at a loss to know how to make his services acceptable there, he is off to the factory. It is the fashion of the day. Excellent priests, those who have a head on their shoulders and know what they are doing, try this method for a definite reason, realizing its limited scope. Their object is, for example, to acquire a better understanding of the worker's mentality; or to bring into the factory a witness, which they know to be exceptional, of priestly brotherhood in work and poverty; or to install the priesthood of Christ in the midst of those who have no idea of what it is. Not so with our ritualist. He throws himself into the adventure with a light heart, although it is an undertaking for which he ought to have exceptional qualities both as a priest and as a man. He goes into it merely because he thinks it is the fashion: nowadays there is no priest worthy of the name who is not a priest-workman. He has none of the spirit which has urged this difficult course on others; he has nothing but the external likeness. The criticism that he draws on himself, the setbacks he suffers, and then the bitterness and irritation he is sure to show, all do their share to throw discredit on an admirable cause.

He also has a genius for emptying of their meaning the words he takes over. Why does he take them over? Always for the same reason: they have an up-to-date ring to them; they go over; they are "the last word." He employs them at random, making them do duty in a hundred different causes; he puts his own private meaning into them, and it is amusing to see the surprising purposes he can make them serve. And so, little by little, discredit falls upon words which, when they were first employed by intelligent men, had a precise and valid meaning; words which, as embodying an inspiration, might have been very fruitful. But now they can be used no longer.

There was, for example, the word "conquest." The Jocists used to speak in 1930 of conquering their

23

brothers, and they meant only that they wanted to win them for Jesus Christ—a meaning which seems to be just as valid twenty years later. But the word has taken on certain overtones which convey the disagreeable suggestion of an injudicious proselytism. Hence you may no longer use it. And the very individual who always had "conquest" on his lips will now give you a condescending smile, or an annoyed look, if you have the bad taste to do so.

Then there was the word "Christendom." [1] We were going to make another Christianity. It was quite a simple thing the word was meant to express: the idea, namely, that the Christian spirit ought to permeate not only individuals alone, but institutions also, environments and social groups and laws insofar as possible. The word, however, also designated a social order which existed in the Middle Ages. Obviously, there was no question of returning to it. But what a temptation there was to glorify that typically Christian era as an ideal! The temptation was not resisted. As a result, the aim of those who wished to build another Christendom was disfigured and they were made to appear visionaries.

There was also the word "*engagement*," [2] with consequent talk of a brand of thinking that was *engagé* and of Christians who were *engagés*. There was nothing

---

[1] The French here is *chrétienté*.

[2] It has been thought better to italicize this word which is hardly at home in English in the sense in which it has lately proved so popular in French—that is, to describe the attitude of one who is not a detached observer, but is willing to, and in fact does, commit himself completely to the causes and movements in which he believes.

wrong with the word at all, since it meant only to express a preference for men who live in contact with real conditions and whose ideas are formed in such contact, rather than for theorists who live isolated in their studies. But along comes our ritualist to appropriate it. He sets himself up to judge the extent of his contemporaries' *engagement*, granting to one man the right to have his say because he is sufficiently *engagé*, while denying it to another because he is not *engagé* enough. *Engagement* is now the only topic of conversation. You have it forever ringing in your ears. The new word gives fresh life to the unending debates on the Christian's part in the temporal domain. You must, however, use the word *engagement*; otherwise, you are behind the times and have no right to be heard. It is so abused that, in the end, we grow tired of the word and then disgusted, and no one will use it any more.

But what of it? We can use "incarnation" in its place. At the moment, this is perhaps the expression which best typifies the spirit we wish to denounce—the tendency, namely, to hypnotize oneself with words. The Incarnation, the Word of God made flesh, is a wonderful reality and one that opens up many avenues of thought: it helps the one who has to preach the word of God to see that, far from being content to expound theological abstractions, he must make the gospel message concrete, incarnating it in everyday language; it helps the Christian to see that his whole life must express the whole of his Christianity; and so on . . . But it sends our friend into an ecstasy of delight. Here he is to tell us that we must become incarnate—even though, to all appearances, this is already a fact. Christ, he tells us, must become incarnate in us (he means that we should reflect the true image of Christ, but his way of saying so is abominable). And so it goes, on and on. In the end, you notice that you can no longer speak of incarnation without causing your companions to wince.

The same is true of the word "testimony." This book, for instance, will be called a "testimony." A testimony of what? Oh, of what the author thinks. What a discovery! Surely when a man has testimony to give, he does not speak of himself but of what he has seen and heard. And the same fate, alas! is in store for the "communitarian spirit" and the "missionary spirit."

Our ritualist transforms words into slogans. For him they are not the signs of realities which he has understood and assimilated; in his mouth they become the passwords and the catchwords of the modern world and the modern apostolate. He ends by making even the most apt and expressive words sound ridiculous, although we need them to spread ideas. This man has a dangerous talent for shrinking values.

We ask you not to confuse the ritualist and the true missionary. The latter will perhaps wear a work shirt, because he thinks it is more practical; he may not always use the best French, because of the environment in which he works; he may be a priest-workman, because this work has been assigned to him; when the situation calls for the words we have discussed, he will use them along with others that he coins himself. But he will never mistake all this for the essence of the missionary apostolate, and he will always put the spirit before the letter and the outward form.

THE PIONEERING SPIRIT

There was a time when Catholics imagined that the real missionary was the man of the jungle and the bush, the man who lived in exotic lands and led a life of escapades, grappling with snakes and panthers, eating unusual food, running rapids in his canoe, and so forth. (To others he was a civilizer, an ambassador of France, an ethnologist. But that is another story.) In the tales they told on returning, the missioners (to suit us, doubtlessly) delighted to dwell on the exotic character of the countries from which they had come back. If our memory of the talks we heard as youngsters does not betray us, little mention was made of the kingdom of God or of the means the missioners had discovered to open the minds of the natives to the gospel. We were no doubt too young to understand. The result has been that for quite a long time the missionary in China or Africa has been considered as an adventurer, and that he himself sometimes shared the idea and set out for the mission field filled with illusions as to what was in store for him.

It was the same story over again when there was question of undertaking the "mission" here in our own country. We were greeted with descriptions of "pioneers" in the Red zone of Paris, these modern explorers being generally welcomed by the fierce inhabitants with a shower of stones. Père Lhande, with his picturesque and moving accounts, succeeded in awaking generous vocations to that very special apostolate. The seminarian who could not see himself at work in the ordinary priestly ministry, as well as the priest of not altogether stable character, found a new career; they felt called to this new work because it was out of the common run, and because in it they would have their freedom and would be doing what others are not. "Here life is monotonous, but there it will be full of excitement. And what heroism it calls for! how sensational it promises to be! and what tales there will be to tell in letters to friends!"

It is the kind of dream the romantic girl has as she finishes the beautiful novel in which the stenographer marries her employer. . . And how drab life seems to her when she goes back to her housework or sets out once more for the office!

Our missionary pioneer finds out even during his apprenticeship that the Red zone is appallingly like the fifteenth *arrondissement*, that the things that make up a priest's life there are just as monotonous as they are elsewhere, and that the word "jungle" is only a metaphor, the image of the same spiritual reality that is everywhere, only more impenetrable. The adventurer type missionary must face the fact that adventure is not found on the street corner; and the reporter type must realize that he will uncover no sensational story to tell. And then, since they do not find what they hoped to find, they are an easy prey to depression.

Amor novitatum is not the missionary spirit; a man is

not called to be a missionary because he loves novelty for the sake of novelty or is always in search of new angles and original approaches or because he needs change for its own sake. The missionary in mission territory, like the apostle in Christian lands, has to do his work in the midst of the simplest realities. His first and foremost ambition is, not to change everything, but to bring Christ to this district, a district that is new only to the missionary himself. Only later will he know whether he must make changes; and then he will not make them as an adventurer would, but as a careful and patient planner, who is guided above all by love.[3]

THE PLANNING SPIRIT

Our next character, the planner or the architect, is at home in this age of the planning board. Recent years have seen the publication of a great number of plans to stabilize the financial situation, to organize the food

---

[3] We cannot do better here than refer to the allocution given by Pius XII to the pastors and preachers of Rome on March 23, 1949. "But always," the Pope said in part, "it will be necessary for the faithful to come together to assist at Mass on Sunday, and the sacraments will always have to be administered to them. And, when we speak of the ministry of souls, we are thinking especially of the sacrament of penance, which requires that the priest should lead an absolutely exemplary life and that he should have a sense of responsibility, clarity and sureness of judgment, self-control, prudence and tact. The poor and the needy, moreover, will always be knocking at the door of the church; there will always be sick people to assist and strengthen by means of the last sacraments; there will always be the deceased, whose funerals will have to be celebrated; the priest will always have to find time for personal conversations with his parishioners . . ."

problem, and to promote world peace. The only thing that remains to be done is to apply them—unless, for having failed to keep in touch with reality, they have already proved themselves inapplicable.

Somewhat the same fate befalls certain desk missionaries. Although they are only second-rate intellectuals, they turn out endless schemes for spreading the gospel systematically. They construct a prefabricated mission without considering the terrain on which they will have to work. They know all there is to know about efficiency. We might represent them as follows: they start by buying the filing cabinet and index cards; then they decide what to write on the cards, only to find that they have nothing to write because they have no documentation on which to draw. Their plans are inapplicable because the authors, when devising them, were out of touch with real life; and above all, because life—especially spiritual life—laughs at plans, for life is the domain of human liberty. It is possible, to be sure, to draw up a four-year plan for equipping a country with airplanes; it is much more difficult to draw up a rational four-year plan of attack on a mission territory. Or rather, nothing is easier than to put such a plan on paper; but when comes time to carry it out, you find that those for whom it was intended are not ready for it and that the co-operation you counted on fails to materialize. Every missioner, of course, makes a plan of campaign and decides on a certain pattern of attack. But when he does so, he works on the basis of the concrete situation as he knows it by experience and on the basis of his knowledge of the road he has already travelled; moreover, he is ready, if the need becomes plain, to change his plans, because he does not attach undue importance to them.

Nor is our planner incapable of altering his views, provided only that he be permitted to remain in the realm of theory. The concrete situation is mobile and always eludes him, but he is even more mobile. What really interests him is drawing up plans. If the first plan does not work, it makes no difference: he will make another. The plans pile up, the actual work is never done. This planner of ours is afflicted with intellectual fidgets. He is continually sending his collaborators, laymen as well as priests, off in new directions, and he always has them panting for breath. After a while, he is amazed to see that there are none to follow him or carry out his orders; instead, following the wise slogan of the barracks, they wait for the orders to be countermanded. He grows impatient and wants to see immediate results. He forgets that many imponderable factors operate in the realm of the spiritual, that the harvest comes long after the sowing, that "one man sows and another reaps." He needs more humility, a greater readiness to adapt himself to reality, and fewer of these ambitious dreams.

The same type of missionary—or his brother, if you like—puts his talent for theorizing at the service of his likes and dislikes. Every man of action feels the need of principles to justify what he is doing. And, like the famous theologian who formulated a thesis and then sent his students to search St. Augustine for texts to support it, our missionary has no scruples about calling theology to his rescue and forcing her to approve his attempts to dodge distasteful work and devote himself to work he likes. If he does not care to visit the sick or his parishioners, to take his turn on duty or at preaching, or even to prepare a sermon, he will not hesitate to go to the Fathers of the Church and to the Scriptures for justification—when a humble examination of conscience would very quickly show him that his lack of mortification is the real reason.

Let us leave to the real thinkers, philosophers or theologians, the task of building up, disinterestedly, the doctrinal source for our work. At the present time we have thinkers we can be proud of, who are in constant contact with men of action and who are giving us a pastoral theology that can be used by every missionary, no matter what type of work he is engaged in. We do better to go to them, bypassing the so-called intellectuals who will (on the basis of new data, new and ephemeral experiences, which they glean here, there, and everywhere) draw up a system on the spur of the moment. These too are architects; they have the best will in the world and are eager to help us. But they are a threat to us, for we may be misled by their incessant flow of plans that are hastily put together and quite insufficiently thought out.

We know them well, these charming confreres. Sometimes they are quite young. They have never put their hand to the plow. They have never really done the work of the ministry. Or, what is worse, they have spent a few weeks or months in it, and are going to live on that "experience" forever afterwards. Still, they have been given, or have taken upon themselves, the responsibility of doing the thinking for those who are actively engaged in the ministry. They listen to a discussion in which men of action, after struggling to see their way clear in the midst of endless complications, have to go home without having reached agreement. But it takes more than that to daunt our confreres. They enter the silence of their study, where their desk provides them with a field of action. Having compared the various points of view, they quickly reach a solution. They emerge triumphant to propose their views, and it never dawns on them that most of the time their discovery is at best a truism.

It must be understood once and for all that the conversion of the world is to be effected otherwise than by sitting down to a typewriter, with a telephone on your right and a filing cabinet behind you. Nothing is more useful than a parish file. Sometimes it is indispensable. Making such a file can afford an extremely valuable examination of conscience on the real state of the parish. But we must be on our guard: once this is completed (and it is never completed, but always in the making), the main thing still remains; and that is to begin the real work, the work of spreading the gospel.

THE SOCIAL-WORKER SPIRIT

Our next type is the man who confuses the role of the missionary with that of the social worker. He would like to make religion popular and to reach souls by looking after bodies. Hence he intends to throw himself into social work, to be an organizer, to start dispensaries, to open placement bureaus, to start a mutual aid society, to organize recreation, and so forth.

It is true that this kind of social work is indispensable. We must have it. Institutions put their stamp on those they work for, marking them with the spirit of the people who take them in hand; it depends on what these people are whether the institutions will prove a beneficial influence in the development of souls or will stifle their spirit. And so we must have Catholics engaged in seeing to it that there is such a thing as Catholic social work.

But is this kind of activity the work of a missionary? On the intellectual plane, in the field of study and theory, it is indispensable to have priests—theologians and historians and even economists—collaborating with laymen in working out a social doctrine (as, for example, in the case of "Economy and Humanism," "Popular Action," the "Social Weeks," and such works). In a diocese, it is normal for a priest to be specially assigned to advise lay people who are engaged in social work. But the priest charged with the care of souls—is it his work to engage personally in this activity? It is better for him to leave this to the laity, whose work it really is —not their only work, as we shall have occasion to point out later, but nevertheless their work.

Otherwise, who is to keep the missionary spirit alive in the parish? Who is to do the actual work of evangelization? Social work is, as we know so well, an absorbing thing, and the man who gives himself to it will soon have no time to announce Christ. He runs the risk of having his activity become, gradually and unknown to himself, quite secular, and of deserting the spiritual for the merely profane. His dispensary will be crowded; children will have been sent off to camp in the mountains; his various activities will be in full swing. Thus he will imagine, too quickly, that his work is done, when in fact there will be so many things left to be done—so many things, or everything, because his real mission work, the work that is his special responsibility, will have yet to begin.

The man who is interested only in typical and rare cases (even in his priestly ministry) is another variety of the missionary-social worker, since his mentality is not unlike that of certain women social workers. He is always on the watch for something out of the ordinary; usual, everyday events and the common run of mortals do not interest him. But he has a passionate interest in difficult spiritual states and complicated spiritual problems. Our "architect" worked with ideas alone when he was drawing up his magnificent plans; but this man limits his activity to the pursuit of individual cases, and he is even capable of framing them to preserve their memory. For him, the ministry consists in gathering data or cases. Does he ever realize that deep down he is working for himself, and not for the good of God's children? He will have to give an accounting for all souls, not only for a few.

THE PROPRIETARY SPIRIT

Have you ever noticed the way the word "consolation" is misused in ecclesiastical literature? People tell a young priest that they hope he will have "many consolations" in his ministry. A prelate speaks of being "greatly consoled" by the fine results he has noted here and there. A pastor congratulates himself on the "many consolations" that a certain portion of his faithful flock gives him, and a big crowd at the Corpus Christi procession seems "especially consoling" to him.

Heaven help us! Do we really find the doing of God's work such a sad business that we need all these sweets to console us in our desolation?

Such must be the mentality of the pseudo-missionary, who is constantly fretting over results, always stealing a glance at his neighbor, and taking note of his success with a certain feeling of bitterness. He wears himself out watching the very slowly ascending—and sometimes descending—curve of his graphs. He would like to harvest, to store up his grain in barns. He is a miser.

Ego plantavi, Apollo rigavit, Deus dat incrementum. It is for God to grant the increase, today or tomorrow or the day after.

You see your neighbor's success, but you do not see the work he has done. You grow tired of your own ministry and you dream of changing places with him; but you never suspect that he too has his difficulties and that the secret of his success lies perhaps in the fact that he works unstintingly and does not worry over results.

On Certain Forms of the Pseudo-Missionary Spirit

When the seventy-two came back overjoyed because their ministry had gone so well, Jesus said to them: "Rejoice not in this, that the spirits are subject to you, but in this, that your names are written in heaven" (Luke 10:20). And you know the words of *Téméraire*: [4] "A man can undertake a task even when he has no hope, and persevere in it even when he has no success." It is true that we have to hope, but with that virtue of hope which envisages the undertaking *sub specie aeternitatis* and puts it in God's hands. We can get along without success, however, for we are called upon, not to succeed, but to work.

It may be providential that there is no harvest for you to reap. If you were to reap, you might perhaps be in danger of becoming set in your ways and of settling down to a life of ease. And that would be the end of everything.

You may dream of the happiness of forming once more a truly "primitive" community, in which you could breathe the very air of the early Christian community. A consolation, indeed, worthy of the name— the kind that appeals to the historian esthete! But if this is your aim and you achieve it and take pleasure in it, you are done for, because you will lose sight of the essential inspiration of the primitive communities: the insatiable desire to extend the boundaries of the kingdom of Christ.

When we search the Acts of the Apostles for inspiration in our missionary work, it is a spirit we are

---

[4] Charles, Duke of Burgundy (fifteenth century).

looking for, not a formula to copy (like a Viollet-le-Duc, when he wanted to reconstruct the cathedral of the Middle Ages). And this spirit is the exact opposite of that proprietary spirit which insists on seeing the harvest. God is the sole proprietor, and He alone has the right to harvest. When we want to usurp God's role, we lose the missionary mentality. Christ reaped no harvest. We will have ours "on the last day when the Lord of the harvest comes." On the last day. Not now.

THE COMPETITIVE SPIRIT

There is another type of missionary in whom the missionary spirit is deficient: the man who lines up his work alongside his neighbor's in a spirit of rivalry. He may do good work in his own bailiwick, but in his eyes everyone else is a competitor, a thorn in his side, perhaps an enemy. When some question arises concerning the Chancery office or the management of parish activities, the district or national directors of the Catholic Action movements or the pastor of the neighboring parish, the religious whom he himself has invited to preach in his parish or the parishioner who has an interest in a supra-parochial movement, you always sense that he is instinctively hostile. He shows it by his conversation and bad humor. His territory is an enclosure where he has every intention of enjoying his extraterritorial rights. The souls in it belong to him. He looks upon himself as the owner of his parish, and his primary concern is that no one but himself should lay a hand on what is his.

He received considerable attention in *Revolution in a*

City Parish; but our picture gallery in this present chapter, were we to omit him, would be incomplete—since this forgetfulness of the kingdom of God (which is implicit in the seeking of one's own kingdom) is the pseudo-missionary spirit in one of its most regrettable forms.

There is an enormous amount of work to be done, and on all sides it reaches beyond the limits of what we might call "our work." If it is to be done, we need the cooperation of every available worker, priest or layman, secular or religious, diocesan and extra-diocesan, local and national. When we have charge of this work in a particular sector, our charge carries with it the responsibility of promoting God's work there with all our strength, and therefore the duty of seeing to it that this work is not compromised by ill-advised or conflicting plans. But it does not give us any right to stifle the Spirit. "Test every spirit and retain what is good."

If our competitor would only read St. Paul again! He would find the Apostle repeatedly reprobating these *aemulationes* and *contentiones*, which are such an obstacle to missionary work precisely because they spring much more from self-love than from love of God.

Paul himself gives us a splendid example of disinterestedness when, as a prisoner in Rome, he writes to the Philippians, among whom all sorts of apostles are working: "Some preach out of envy, to compete against me. They are prompted by a spirit of rivalry and think that they are increasing the sorrows of my chains. It matters not: in any case, whether through hypocrisy or sincerely, Christ is proclaimed. I rejoice in this and I will always rejoice in it."

The pseudo-mystic is likely to be found among those who have already been in the active ministry for several years. He has tried everything (at least he thinks so!) and he has not succeeded. Can it be that he has failed to grasp this fact: that the first thing to do is to reform himself, his ideas, and his life? He has devoted himself to the reform of externals, and the externals offered resistance. And now he is cynical.

There are different ways of being cynical. Sometimes a man becomes bitter and makes up for his disappointments by laughing at others and being critical of their work; and he is a cause of discouragement to them.

The pseudo-mystic, though, has his own way. He canonizes his desire to escape from it all. "If I have not succeeded," he says, "it is because God does not want me to succeed. Now I understand my vocation: it is to be a failure. There is no use saying anything. I will retire to a life of silence and prayer. There is no need for me to be upset: God is using my failure for His own ends."

There is no doubt the man means well. He speaks that way, but is he quite sure he is not making the will of God responsible for his own mistakes in procedure, his own tactical errors, his own personal shortcomings, and now for the cowardly desertion which leads him to abandon a task that has become too heavy for him? How does he know that God wants to work through his

40

failure? To be sure of it, he would have to have a personal revelation. If he restricts himself to the revelation that is the property of all—and is all that counts when you want to stay on the right track—God wants to work, not through his success, but through his labor.

As long as there is a breath of life in us, it is our duty to use it on the work we have to do. And that work is: the actual labor itself, a spiritual task of prayer and sacrifice and a task of thinking over and repeatedly reconsidering the form our activity is taking. Suppose we have failed—it is much too easy to say that God does not will our success, and much more likely that we have not gone about our work properly. We must retrace our steps, go back to the intersection where we probably took the wrong road, have the courage to look for the new roads that are still open to us. That means we must observe what others are doing, and pay more attention to the needs of the people under our care and to the possible openings which the grace of God might find to enter their souls. Besides, it means we must pray more fervently for light.

THE PSEUDO-ANGELIC SPIRIT

We have used strong language to denounce those priests who allow themselves to be absorbed by work which is not theirs, by manual work, by dramatic and sporting organizations, by administrative and financial activities. Hence we have the right to present the other side of the picture too.

There is a type who would overspiritualize the apos-

41

tolate and avoid any work which is not purely priestly and missionary. In the end, such a man loses sight of a certain number of things to which, whether he likes it or not, he must submit if he is to accomplish anything in this base world.

There is a principle that we should "do nothing that is not purely priestly." Our angelic missionary uses it for all—and more than all—that it is worth. With that to back him, he rises to such heights that he will no longer even touch the earth with his foot, nor will he stoop to raise, even with the tip of his little finger, the burdens which others (his fellow workers) will have to carry for him.

Woe to the pastor who has the bad luck to have such an assistant! The parish may be having a fair or a bazaar. Every now and then it may be necessary for someone to put a room in order for a catechism class, to arrange the chairs for an unforeseen meeting, to start a fire, or to see to the transportation of the baggage when some group is going to camp. In an emergency it may be necessary to call upon someone to do some typing or mimeographing in order to prepare announcements for a meeting; someone may even have to take his bicycle and distribute them without delay. There are the decorations to be improvised for a popular feast, and the plans to be made for a liturgical ceremony. It is just too bad for his confreres, and for the success of the undertaking too, if anyone is counting on this assistant. This gentleman has declared that he will not waste his time

42

on such things. It is up to his fellow assistants or to his pastor to look after them if they wish to.

Generally it is with disdain that he refuses to have any part in such things, but at times he may take refuge behind an argument which renders him invulnerable. In order to have the right to play the angel, he will have no qualms about playing dumb and warning you that he knows nothing at all about such things, that he is awkward and out of his element, that he would not know where to start. Nor will he hesitate, if it helps the cause, to intone a hymn of admiration for his more gifted associates, though it may only be a question of taking a broom to sweep out a room or of going into the church to see that all the people have their books.

And when his associates are doing their best to arrange schedules, plan decorations, and see to it that the services will go off well, he continues his spiritual occupations unmoved. His life is affected by Christmas Eve and Corpus Christi only to the extent that he has to spend more time in the confessional; but he is able to prepare his sermon in peace, while the others must prepare theirs in advance or try to do it in the rush of preparations for so many other things.

But you, his beloved associates, must not be downcast. You will have the comfort of seeing him come in at the last moment, his mind and face in repose, and quite surprised that the commotion is not yet at an end. Woe to you, however, if in the course of the ceremony or the meeting it turns out that you have forgotten something or failed to foresee some contingency. It is a safe bet that our angelic missionary will be the first to complain of your lack of foresight and to protest against your sad incapacity to cover it up.

It is true that we ought to leave the greatest possible share of the manual work to lay people when they can replace us. And when it is question of work of this kind, we are justified in following the well-known barracks slogan: "Never do today what someone else can do tomorrow"—but on condition that the someone else is not an associate who has just as much work to do as we have.

Yet we should not forget that the faithful who are tied down by this material work are not doing the work of the apostolate any more than the priest would be. They, as well as we, can be seriously tempted to abandon the urgent and necessary work of Catholic Action to take refuge in occupations which require much less effort and self-mastery. When we use laymen for this kind of work, we are simply transforming them into church employees.

Nor should we forget that in an ideal, perfectly organized parish, the priests would not have to bother with these material affairs, or that a committee for church celebrations can assume much of the clergy's burden in such matters. But until the day comes when the priest has his eyes and his hands altogether free, he will inevitably have jobs to do which will force him to roll up his sleeves, dirty his hands, and sometimes tear his cassock. It is a fortunate pastor who has curates with courage to knuckle down to these jobs, ingenuity to do them well, simplicity to do them with a smile.

If we went on with portraits of this kind (which we very well could do), we would meet the *journalist*, whose mind is on nothing but book reviews and convention reports; the *pontiff*, whose life work is to see that his dignity is respected; the *esthete*, the *gourmet*, and many others. And even when we had pinned up our collection of specimens, we should not have exhausted the reality, since the weeds spring up all too easily in the poor soils of our souls. Why do we produce so many weeds? Can we explain it by the defective training given our young men? Are not these aberrations from the missionary spirit a reaction against repression? The young priest has heard so much criticism of fresh initiatives, he has been warned so often against dangerous tendencies, his aspirations have been so stifled, he has been under such pressure that he lets off steam wherever he can find an outlet. In his experience there have been too many ukases and too many prohibitions, all of them laid down without sufficient explanation. All the deviations we have pointed out betray a lack of missionary spirit and an absence of authentic missionary principles. But in certain forms of attachment to tradition and to things as they are, is there not the same lack of missionary spirit and principles? Drawing up a list of deformities and banning them does not cure them. You can cure them only by changing the spirit that begot them.

From the start of this book, we have insisted on drawing up an indictment of varieties of the pseudo-missionary spirit or of possible deviations from the missionary spirit. But the reader may be sure that we have done so not for the perverse pleasure of criticizing nor with any idea of making common cause with the complacent and the satisfied. We wanted to do it for two reasons. In the first place, to dissociate the missionary cause from those individuals who are discrediting it by their excesses and exposing it to condemnations unfair to the majority of missionaries. And in the second place, to warn our younger brothers (and ourselves first of all) of the pitfalls we shall all, to a greater or lesser extent, find in our path, because it is into these that we run the risk of falling.

Finally, at the end of this court trial, we may sum up its positive aspect. The thing to emphasize, always and endlessly, is the missionary spirit, which is nothing but the authentic apostolic spirit. We must never let ourselves be taken in by externals—by methods or words, attitudes or so-called consolations, results or theories or prestige. We must never seek ourselves, but only the kingdom of God and his justice, being constantly eager to serve, here where we are and with all that we are, in total submission to the guiding hand of Providence and the unfailing stimulus of charity. *Caritas Christi urget nos.*

III

On the Need of Having Something to Replace What We Destroy

We might have sketched another portrait, entitled "The Wrecker," and added it to those in the preceding chapter. It would have represented the missionary who has but one ambition on arriving in a new locality—to make a clean sweep of everything his predecessors have done.

Some readers of *Revolution in a City Parish*, readers who went through the book in a hurry, picking out a paragraph here and there, may have imagined that this was the method we championed; they may accordingly have praised us for it and claimed us for their side; or, on the other hand, they may have charged it up against us.

After all, this age of ours is one of reconstruction, one that is so perforce because of the war bombings. Are we not accustomed to seeing reconstruction jobs getting their start everywhere by a demolition job? We take advantage of our misfortunes to rebuild on new lines; and, when needs be, we do not hesitate to tear down buildings that are still intact, in order to carry out a city plan providing for model neighborhoods.

We might even push the analogy further and remark that there is sometimes a danger for the tenants who happen to be involved in these splendid city plans and who, because of these plans, see the time when they will be decently lodged removed to the far distant future.

But let it suffice to say that souls must never be treated as if they were stones, nor the field of the father of the family as a lot on which we are to be continually rebuilding. The Lord does not send us to perform experiments, but to do His work. We have no right to make tests *in anima vili*, to see what the outcome may be, at the risk of making our parishioners suffer; we must not be like those unscrupulous doctors and surgeons who experiment on their hospital patients. Even in the hypothesis that our fellow workers would learn from our tests and derive profit from them, such tests are not permissible, because the end does not justify the means. The hypothesis, besides, is a purely imaginary one, because what proves a success in one place turns out a failure in another, and vice versa.

Missionary work is not done in the clouds or in the realm of a priori considerations. Our task is to bring our priesthood into a definite area which the Father has entrusted to us just as it is. We can visualize our parish as we imagine it will one day be, rather than as it really is; we can—but doing so is a bad mental habit. There may quite well be something wrong with the situation we find on our arrival; and, if so, we shall certainly have to make changes. But we must not decide in the abstract what these changes should be; we must begin rather with what already exists and proceed from there to make things better. What that "better" thing actually is will gradually become clear to us as we acquire a better knowledge of our people, their possibilities, the things they are most attached to, and their special needs.

We should like to take the liberty of borrowing some of the Marxist thesis on the historical process. We cannot make history, or influence its course, by attempting to impose prefabricated views on our contemporaries, without taking into account the existing historical situation. We must accept reality and take our place in it if we want to have an influence on its evolution. In other words, what we have to do is to inject a spirit into all the concrete realities and existing institutions which present themselves to us. Those that have life in them will absorb this spirit and serve as a vehicle for it; those that have seen their day will waste away of themselves, and others will take their place. Our job is not to destroy, but to build. And the new structures we raise, if they are really what is needed, will make the old ones fall apart.

What we as priests have to do is to put God into a given part of this world. The only previous consideration which helps the priest in this task is his determination to love all his parishioners unselfishly, without excluding or favoring any of them—a determination, that is, to love them as Christ desires to love them through us. The main thing is not to organize a district according to our way of seeing things; the main thing is to make it an offering to God, while at the same time we ask Him to give us His light and His love so that we may be enabled to transform it in the way He wants it transformed.

This is all the more true because, when we do find in a parish something that has to be changed or that displeases us, although it may well be due to abuses or ignorance and ineptitude, it is much more probably due to historical, social, or geographic factors we are unaware of. At any rate, the parish, in the state we find it both as regards the people and the activities, is our inheritance from those who have preceded us. The people are not to be blamed if their formation has been incomplete or faulty. Most of them have carried out in good faith the directions given them. It is not their fault if our predecessors asked too much or too little of them. Our duty is to accept the inheritance lovingly and with a grievance against no one, to accept it in order to make it bear fruit, not to destroy it. Furthermore, if we love persons and not institutions, souls and not our own kingdom, we shall have no difficulty in welcoming all of our people just as they are.

Some examples from parish life will illustrate our point.

CHURCH RECREATION CENTERS

Church nurseries are not, in our opinion, effective as a missionary method of reaching the children—a view which we explained at sufficient length in *Revolution in a City Parish*. As we see it, our priestly activity should not be primarily centered on the children, but rather on the adults.

Does this mean that we think there is no need to bother with the children, or that, on arriving in a parish, our first act should be to abolish the recreation center? God forbid!

In many a parish, the various recreational activities extend all the way from those for very small children to those for older girls. The only solidly established organizations in the parish, they have this at least in their favor—they exist. We need not look upon them as forever sacrosanct. Deep in our hearts we may definitely prefer other more apostolic and more fruitful forms of activity. But it will take time for these other forms to come into being, and in the meantime we must make use of these recreations—not with bad grace, letting everyone know that we are not interested and are going through with them simply out of a sense of duty and for lack of something better to do; no, but using them wholeheartedly and sincerely. If we bring a missionary spirit to this kind of work and succeed in injecting it into these activities, it is quite natural that the members of such groups will eventually hunger for something more, and the time will then have come for us to introduce new forms and new ideas.

Father Rétif has already explained in some detail the work he proposes to do with the children, both while they are attending catechism and afterwards.[1] We will mention briefly what is being done; it is certainly not definitive, but, like everything else in the missionary life, is being continually adapted.

Let us take our parish at Grand Colombes as an example. The priest in charge of the recreation center there soon noticed two things. First, that most of the children who kept up the practice of their religion did not come to the recreation center; second, that the center did not afford him opportunity to have on the children an influence deep enough or priestly enough to satisfy him. He continued to spend his Thursday afternoons at the recreation center until the children began of their own accord to gather in small neighborhood groups, called "gangs." There is already a considerable number of children in them. The priest has enlisted the aid of several of the youngsters, and now spends all day Thursday passing from one gang to another. That he never thought he should get the children off his hands is clear from the fact that he now gives them a greater part of his Thursday than he formerly gave to the recreation center. The only difference is that he has restricted his activity to what is essentially priestly.

And so too with the priest who works with the little girls. He has no recreation center, but the same system of small groups (called "circles" by the girls) certainly enables him to reach more children than did the recreation center.

The results are not ambiguous. Every year the number

---

[1] Cf. "Catéchisme et mission ouvrière" in the series *Rencontres*.

of those who turn out for both retreats (one at the beginning of the school year and the other at Easter) is very large in relation to the number of those making their solemn Communion. In one of the worst sections of our parish at Petit Colombes, for example, we observed that there was not a single deserter at the end of a year, and two or three at the most the following year.

From this, there can clearly be no question of abandoning the children; on the contrary, we must think of all and take in hand every soul in the parish as efficiently as possible.

We would never dream of giving up recreation centers and parish activities if we had nothing to put in their place. Our conscience would give us no peace if we did not see to it that the children as well as the adults were having the gospel preached to them.

THE QUESTION OF THE SOLEMN COMMUNION

The question of the solemn Communion illustrates even better what we have been saying. A great deal of criticism has been levelled at this ceremony. And rightly so. Generally everything connected with it is a lie: the words ("first," which is false, and "solemn," which is meaningless); the speeches, which pretend to believe in tomorrows that will never exist; the renewal of the baptismal promises made by children who are not old enough to make any commitments; the mentality of so many parents, who accede to our demands only for the sake of the family celebration in which the main thing is the meal, the costume, and the presents.

Since this is so, should we abolish the solemn Communion? Some think so, and it is precisely the love of truth that motivates them. Father Remillieux, of whom we thought so much, was one of these.[2] Gradually he succeeded in replacing this ceremony with another of quite different form, a ceremony whose preparation permitted him a very interesting contact with the families of his parish.

If we disagree with this procedure, it is because we look at the situation from another angle. It has been our experience that the first solemn Communion is the only religious event left which, without our having to work up the interest of the people, creates a stir in the dechristianized environments in which our work lies. This is the one time in the entire year that we do not have to attract the people; they come of themselves in such numbers that we never know where to put them. They come—all kinds: good Catholics and non-Christians, friends of the family and members of the parish. This is a fact. This is the real situation.

Of course, we accomplish nothing at all if, on this occasion, we simply fill ourselves with pleasant ("consoling") illusions and deliver sentimental sermons punctuated with insipid and unreal hymns. Do this, and we simply become ridiculous, to the detriment of religion in general and of those who attend the ceremony.

But before the first Communion takes place, it can be an occasion for us to visit the families of the children; to organize meetings of their parents, in the course of

---

[2] Cf. "Notre-Dame Saint-Alban" in the series *Rencontres*, ch. IV.

which we can touch on problems of living that are as important to the parents as to the children; and finally, to cultivate public opinion by preparation for the big day. That is an excellent opportunity for missionary work. As for the day itself, there is nothing to prevent our looking upon it as a chance for a splendid introductory ceremony for the benefit of all those half-Christians who will be with us morning and evening. There is nothing to prevent our directing our sermon at them rather than at the children. The promise the children make at the evening ceremony will be nothing but make-believe, if we encourage the pretense that it commits them for life. But there is nothing to prevent our cutting it down to their size and making it concern the more immediate future; nor is there anything to prevent our asking the parents to join in it.

Neither does this promise, adapted to the age of the children, in any way preclude the possibility of a more serious pledge several years later when, as adolescents, they will know what they are doing.

Let us suppose for a moment that this institution did not exist at all, and that we had neither the solemn Communion nor the instructions that lead up to it. What would be left to us, in most of our parishes, in the way of opportunities for giving religious instruction to the children or even for making contact with their parents?

Let us also suppose that somewhere in France (where, in the hypothesis, nothing of the kind existed) a pastor conceived an idea. It consisted in a yearly ceremony which enabled him to round up most of the twelve-year-olds, together with their parents and an army of relatives. Furthermore, it enabled him to have the children meet with him every week for three years with their parents' consent. Let us suppose further that this priest is clever enough to succeed in making this ceremony so much a part of life that it becomes a custom. The stores mark it by special displays; the public schools respect it; even the indifferent have come to look upon it with a certain sympathy. In short, let us suppose he does his work so well that this ceremony becomes a social event. Every priest in the country would come to admire this ingenious pastor and to interrogate him, and everyone who wanted to be a missionary would copy him.

Now it is just such a situation that exists among us and has passed into the category of a custom. We must not overestimate it; we must never imagine that it has more value than it actually has. We must put life into it if it is showing signs of old age, but let us not destroy it for the pleasure of destroying.

Likewise, we have no illusions concerning the efficacy of the catechism, that famous catechism which we have to teach the children as preparation for first Communion. We know very well that they will not retain one word of the catechism and that religion is not a subject which can be "taught" the same way as arithmetic. But, since we know this is so, why should we not take advantage of these years of preparation to accomplish something at once more fundamental and more genuine?

On this point there is no need to elaborate, since Father Rétif has just published in this same series a work entitled *Catechism and the Worker Mission,* which treats the subject from every angle and to which we refer our readers.[3]

THE CARE OF THE SICK

Just as some question the value of the first solemn Communion, others question the current practice in regard to the sacrament of the sick.

"Here you have people," they say, "who have lived their whole lives outside the Church, people whose lives have been wholly uninfluenced by religion. Now their last hour has come. They are hardly conscious perhaps. In any case, they know nothing about the nature of the sacrament they are going to receive. And often they protest against the priest's visit. What am I supposed to do for them? I will have no part in this sham of administering a sacrament which will not mean anything."

This they use as a pretext for refusing to go see the sick who do not call them, putting forward the claim that they do not wish to exert any imprudent pressure on people and prefer to leave the sick their liberty. They save themselves for people who are in the full flower of life and who are of so much greater importance.

We agree that we should never force the sacrament on anyone underhandedly, because this sacrament, like the others, has no magical or automatic power. Yet it is only when the sacrament has been explicitly refused that we are forbidden to administer it. Whenever there is a possibility that it is desired, even if there has been no sign of this desire, we are obliged to administer it.

With much greater reason—and this is the point we

---

[3] "Catéchisme et mission ouvrière" in the series *Rencontres*.

wish to stress—can we be charged with failing gravely in our duty if we neglect visiting the sick, even if we neglect only those who are not practicing Catholics or who are hostile to the Church. It is not a question of capturing them or of adding another name to our pious list of conquests. It is an obligation of our missionary apostolate which we have to the sick as to all, though our obligation to the sick is a more urgent one because they are so soon to appear before God. "Father, of those whom thou hast given me, I have not lost one." We must be able to say that to the Father when He asks us for an accounting; we must be able to say, "No one has been lost through my fault." The Lord has poured out His blood for this sick person who has lived so far from Him. We still have a chance to make him understand this, to let him glimpse that eternity which is now so close to him. We may not be able to give him the sacrament, but the words with which we prepare him for a good death may be the means of starting in him an imperceptible interior movement that will open up to him the arms of Mercy.

The true missionary is not fastidious about the exercise of his ministry: he grasps every opportunity that offers itself. And this work with the sick is obviously one of the most urgent tasks of the ministry.

THE PARISH MILIEU

The reader may recall the way we used this term in *Revolution in a City Parish*. It served to describe the parish as made up of the restricted circle of those

Catholics who, though practicing and devout, have no missionary outlook at all, but are quite content with things as they are and quite attached to their own way of doing things. They are a threat to the clergy because they tend to make the parish priests prisoners within their "consoling" and suffocating circle, isolating them from the great masses who are left to go about their business with no one to care for them.

We said, and at sufficient length, that the missionary had to fear being taken over by this narrow group, that he had to go beyond it and reach the rest of the people. Does this mean that we must cast these Catholics of long standing into the outer darkness or that we cannot bother with them? Must we tell them that their reign is over and that we have something else to do besides spending our time on them?

God forbid! To begin with, they have souls as well as anyone else—souls which we must look after. They constitute our inheritance, and it is our duty to pick up the work of our predecessors where they left off. Such people generally have the best will in the world; and, although it is difficult, it is not impossible to win them over to the missionary cause. After all, they are the first field of activity open to us. They are there—there, just as the Jews of the synagogues of the Dispersion were. And God knows how unwilling those Jews were to receive the new dispensation that Paul was preaching to them and how they threw all their weight against him in his resolve to convert the Gentiles. Yet, not only did Paul

59

always begin with them, but he made many converts and found many useful collaborators among them.

The parish milieu has to be transformed, but it must not be neglected. How can we reach these people? The virtue of religion offers us a starting point. Since non-Christians are more easily reached through the evangelical and social aspects of Christianity, we can use these means to bring them around to the sphere of religion proper. Traditional Catholics, on the other hand, have a sense of piety, a realization of their duty to God. But God is the Father of every one of us; Mary is the Mother of the human race; Christ is the universal Redeemer. They have a great devotion to the Sacred Heart, even if it is not always as enlightened a devotion as it might be. All these facts represent so many avenues by which they may be led to an evangelical and social view of the world—provided we start with what is, if not very real to them, at least very familiar. If we can get them to see that their desire for the kingdom includes and implies the apostolate and that they cannot love God without loving their fellow men, we are doing missionary work.

Moreover, the parish milieu is not made up solely of fervent Catholics or even of Catholics who habitually practice their religion. On its fringes there is also an important group of people who once went to catechism, who made their Communion, were married in the Church, and who now send us their children. To them also Christianity has only one aspect: the "religious." The normal thing is for this group to give the mission its first conquests; it is among them that our visits first bear fruit and that our liturgically inspired ceremonies can count on winning sympathizers. Not that we are to concentrate on them exclusively, since this would cut us off very quickly from the pagan masses who are even more important. But we must do serious work among them. And once they are touched by grace, they have the mettle to make good leaders in the pagan environment to which they are closer than most other people.

When we speak thus, we are taking the risk of being a little too jubilantly approved by persons who have never broken out of the parish milieu and tried to reach those beyond that circle. So much the worse for those who understand us so! Now, more than ever, are we convinced that it is precisely those "others" who must be the preferred object of our missionary apostolate, since it is they who are the lost sheep. Now, more than ever, are we convinced that we must preach the gospel to the whole world, not just to a small group that is already organized. But it is "with Jerusalem, Judea, and Samaria" that we must begin; and these too, despite appearances, need to be reached by the missionary movement.

THE MISSIONARY HIMSELF

The conclusion is that the true missionary of Jesus Christ, when considering his work, ought never to think of what he has to destroy, but only of what he has to build.

Let us now take a further step. All the demands we make on him in his personal life, if it is to be that of a real missionary, must be considered—not under their negative, but under their positive, aspect—as demands that spring from the very depths of our priesthood.

There is, for example, the question of priestly poverty. The priest has to be poor. But why? So as not to shock the workers. So as to be in tune with his people, who are poor. This is the first reason that comes to our minds, and there is truth in it. But if this were the only answer, the whole answer—would it not be a kind of trick, this poverty of ours: a trick to curry favor? Moreover, as an argument it would be extremely feeble if our people happen to be for the most part middle-class. The truth is that, if we must be poor, it is because Christ was poor, because the Apostles were poor, because the gospel beatifies poverty, because the very nature of our priesthood demands that we should renounce the goods of this world. We have to be poor in order to be free, free to be priests of Jesus Christ and nothing else, free to be available for every type of missionary apostolate.

Then there is the matter of the priestly community of life and work. Beyond a doubt, we champion the community as an indispensable means of sustaining our fervor and of supporting ourselves in our work. But here again it seems to us that community life and work are demanded by the very nature of the priesthood. If we read the Acts of the Apostles again, we will see that there are always several gospel preachers together. They do not act individually. It is a group that announces Christ. A body of assistants takes shape around the bishop, and this forms the core of the Church of such and such a place. The same phenomenon is reproduced again and again in the history of the first centuries. Communities of presbyters are the rule. And every time there has been a renewal of life in the Church, a resurrection of community life has been part of it. St. Augustine is a case in point. Not that we are to copy or even transpose a way of life taken from the Acts of the Apostles or the Constitutions of St. Augustine—it is the spirit behind them that we have to discover and make our own. And what is that spirit? Nothing but charity and fraternal love, for this is the very essence of the missionary spirit.

Often enough we say that we must make the laity do their part, and not do everything ourselves. But our purpose should not be merely to give them something to keep busy with or to put them into the game so that they will feel useful, whereas we feel all the time that we could get along quite well without their help. If this is our attitude (like that of a mother who makes her little daughter quite proud by assigning part of the housework to her, though it will all have to be done over later), we are acting in that frame of mind which we have called negative. We give the laity only such jobs as are purely material, and even then we keep an eye on them all the time. We mistrust their initiative and are always on our guard to see that they do not take anything upon themselves. We treat them as perpetual minors. All in all, we give them dolls to play with while we are taking care of the serious business.

We have to get away from this paternalistic and clericalist attitude. When we say that we must make the laity our associates in the apostolate, we mean that they have a mission of their own in the Church. We mean that they have a part to play which derives from their very nature as persons whom baptism has made members of Christ the Priest. It is their "priesthood" we have in mind. They have a work of their own to do; it is not ours, and we must hand it over to them with complete readiness and confidence.

There is, in the first place, all that material work of which we as priests ought to free ourselves. We recall here the example of a cathedral pastor. He has divided the affairs of his parish into five categories (schools, vacation camps, secretarial work, and so forth), and has entrusted the management of each category to a committee. He started by entrusting to them the administration of all *expenditures* in connection with schools: salaries, furniture, repairs, books, etc.; and automatically the *income* increased three hundred per cent, so quick were the people of the parish to catch the idea.

But there is spiritual work for them too—the work, for example, of directing the liturgical ceremonies, of organizing neighborhood meetings, of directing activities in a workers' section. Again, there is the work of participating in a missionary campaign, as did the laity in the mission of Briey or la Creuse or l'Yonne,[4] etc. It is

---

[4] In these three districts of France there were recently conducted parish missions according to a somewhat new plan. All the parishes of a district, as many as thirty or forty, had a mission going on at the same time. Part of the plan was to bring the mission before the eyes and ears of the public by an extensive publicity campaign, and in this the laity played a prominent part.

obvious, of course, that we are never going to turn over to them the entire work of spreading the gospel, and that we must constantly supervise them in order to see that their teaching is sound and their methods prudent; otherwise, we would risk heresy and anarchy. But, on the other hand, we must never look on them as mere errand boys, and never refuse to allow them initiative or give them responsibility. The positive work of the priest in this matter consists in creating a laity. Were he to be content with making some concessions to them, his action would be purely negative.

The same principles apply in the ticklish question of politics. "No politics" is our advice to the priest; it is the advice of the entire hierarchy too. This advice, however, may be taken quite negatively; and, so understood, it would differ little from the ideal of the lay state. Politics is a field of human activity, and nothing that is human can exclude Christ altogether. This advice therefore means that no stand is to be taken in purely political questions in which men are free to make up their own minds, and that we should not, as priests, interfere in a domain in which the faithful have a right to their liberty. It is easy to see how far this transcends any cheap opportunism, which would have us avoid offending anyone so that we might win everyone. The priest, by the very fact that he is a priest, is the father of all and belongs to all; it is inherent in the priesthood to be above human quarrels. Yet, at the same time, political activity is human activity; and the priest must constantly be forming men who will be capable of fighting as Christians in the state, so that through them the state may be the city of God.

We could give many more examples. But these will suffice to bring out our main thought: that the demands which the missionary priesthood makes on us should not be envisaged as a series of almost negative concessions to what is called for by the spirit and the conditions of our times, but rather should be thought of as springing directly from the priestly spirit itself. If we are to make the fullest use of our priesthood and bear the fruit we should bear, our priesthood must be poor and communitarian; it must have the laity as its associates; and so on. The most urgent work of all is to provide true priests —priests who will neither be content with things as they are without taking the trouble to reflect on them, nor, on the other hand, throw themselves into the apostolate with the crude notion of turning everything upside down; but priests who will be so conscious of their priesthood and of what God wants from them and from the world in which they live that they will instinctively discover how they ought to conduct themselves and what work they ought to take up.

IV

The Essence of the Missionary Spirit

We had, at first, to clear up false notions about the missionary and point out that his work is positive rather than negative. It is now time to pass to the main theme: to ask ourselves what the missionary spirit—as we envisage it—really is, and to draw up a general outline of a missionary spirituality.

We will start with the missionary spirit, which to us seems composed of a threefold vision: a vision of the world, a vision of the Church, a vision of the love of Christ.

VISION OF THE WORLD

To make ourselves better understood we are going to use a modern illustration and compare the missionary spirit with the spirit of a convinced Communist militant. But note that we are confining our observations to the field of psychology. We are making no comparison between communism and Christianity. Such a comparison, as we know only too well, is bound to do less than justice to the true nature of Christianity. Christianity is no socio-economic theory, but something else altogether, something so transcendent that we cannot lay it alongside human theories. Our comparison, therefore, bears on states of mind, and on these alone.

A Man of Conviction

It is a fact that the militant Communist, surrounded as he is by all sorts of opportunists with no convictions at all, bases his action on a philosophy (we came near saying "a theology") of the world, a philosophy which has breadth. His actions may give the impression that he is only a shortsighted politician, and he may seem to be constantly shifting his ground. But these changing positions have no effect on his creed. On the contrary, they are dictated by his creed—the Marxist concept of historical development. This is a development which is inescapably moving toward the establishment of universal communism; and universal communism is the condition of human well-being and happiness. In the light of the historical materialism of Karl Marx and Lenin, the Communist sees the world of tomorrow which is even now in the making. He has his plan. He knows where he is going and where the world is going. His gospel has told him these things.

Let us be honest enough to admit that we cannot say as much of many Catholics or even of many priests. They are the custodians of a tradition, the formulas of which they discreetly repeat. Still, can it be said that they are carried away and almost entranced by a world vision that is their own? They are the heirs of a past; but they are not builders of the future, because they do not appreciate the full magnificence of Christianity. They preach a moral system; they even preach dogmatic truths; but they are not heralds proclaiming the only Word of God.

The real missionary is, if anything, just such a herald. He is the messenger of the living Word, whose name is Jesus Christ. He too has his view of history. To him history is the kingdom of God being born in pain and sorrow. To him it is not the story of a past for which he sadly longs, but the story of the Cross, its preparation and its glorious reality: *stat Crux dum volvitur orbis*. He too has a solid body of doctrine as the cornerstone of his life; it is the gospel of Jesus Christ, and he is completely obsessed by it. For him, too, the world in general, and with all its ups and downs, is moving toward an end to which it is also carrying us. That end is the second coming of Christ, without which it is impossible to make sense out of the world and its movement. In his body of doctrine there are immense riches: the Mystical Body of Jesus Christ singing the praises of God; the divine life, which glorifies and elevates the life of men; the universal love that comes from the Father and goes back to the Father; the Easter message that the world is saved because the risen Jesus is ever moving through our midst and carrying us along with Him toward the happiness that is to be ours. And it is more than a message, for the God-Man is really living in our midst and inviting us to be united with one another in Him. What are objections and controversies, or even shortcomings and setbacks, in comparison to the Word of God Incarnate in Christ, that Word which never ceases to resound in the missionary's ears? He knows where he is going and where the world is going. He has been swept off his feet by the beauty and the magnificence of the universal salvation which it is his mission both to proclaim and to translate into reality. This, surely, is far removed from the didacticism of tracts and catechism and codes of moral precepts.

The psychological state of the missionary is that which St. John describes for us at the beginning of his first Epistle: "What we have heard, what we have seen with our eyes, what we have looked upon, what our hands have touched—and the life also has been manifested and we have seen it and we bear witness to it . . . we announce it to you also that you may be in communion with us. For your communion is with the Father and with his Son Jesus Christ. And we write these things in order that your joy may be perfect. . . . The news that we announce to you is that God is light . . ."

It is possible to read between the lines here and detect what an overwhelming experience it had been for St. John to come into contact with Christ, of whose life he was a witness. It had been an overwhelming experience for him that day when he first met Him who was the Messias and who was bearing the sins of the world, that day when John first came to see the sins of the world through Christ's eyes. After that, he could no longer

70

look at the world without thinking of its sins and without taking upon himself the burden of its sins.

It had been an overwhelming experience for him to hear Christ announcing the Beatitudes and telling the parables. After that, he was haunted by the need to preach those Beatitudes and to see them put into practice; he was dominated by the passion for the kingdom that lived in him both as an unfading dream and as the only worth-while reality.

It had been an overwhelming experience for him to see Christ working miracles, and to know that he was in the presence of God and was touching God ("what our hands have touched"); but it had given him confidence in that divine power, which would not stop short of miracles, and the conviction that God would be with him when he was doing God's work.

It had been an overwhelming experience for St. John and the Apostles to witness Christ's Passion and death and to feel their own human lives falling to pieces along with Him. But the supremely overwhelming experience for him had been to see Jesus risen from the dead, to see Him ascend into heaven, and to receive the revelations of Pentecost. Yes, it was an overwhelming experience, one that struck him like a bolt of lightning; but one that shed its light on everything, on his own life, on life in general, on the world. "The news is that God is light."

This is the ferment that gives the heart of the missionary no rest. This is the passion that agitates him. This is the vision he has of the world; and, once he has

71

it, he cannot rest unless he is bringing to others that same light and power and vision.

A Realist

Though his adversaries may consider his vision of the world Utopian, the militant Communist is a realist all the same. He has eyes for more than history and the general direction it is taking. He never takes his eyes off what is happening around him and in the world at large, and he sees that things are not what they should be. He is obsessed by the suffering of others, which for him is a reality. He sees injustice in the relative situations of both the underdog and the profiteer. He sees the injustice and he does not reconcile himself to it. He is not content with the things that are, as they are; in fact, every detail of things as they are is, in his eyes, an aspect of the evil he wants to do away with. If you invite him to conform, he answers you with facts. Facts, always facts—this is a characteristic of every Communist argument. And it accounts in part for the strength of communism, because, while it is quite possible to discuss theories, facts are there in front of you, hitting you between the eyes. You must concede that they exist, before you can begin to interpret them.

It is a rather curious paradox that people who pride themselves on being the least Utopian are also the least realistic. But on second thought it is not surprising: they are not hungry, and so they are the first to have enough. Let us imagine an apostle who lacks the missionary spirit. He will be content to hold on at any cost to things as they are; at the same time, he will be very quick to say, "Let us have no exaggeration. It is not as bad as all that." If you tell him, "Look here! there are already four hundred Adventists in this little city of ours, and they are taking quite a few people from us," he will give you a smile of pity and reply, "At Easter our cathedral was crowded at all the Masses." He picks up a magazine and reads two articles, one of which sets forth the distressing figures showing the progress of dechristianization, while the other lists the number of Easter communions in the *grandes Écoles*.[1] The first article will shock him slightly when he reads it, but his memory will make a place only for the figures of the second article. Realities escape him —spiritual realities even more successfully than statistical ones. He fails to see what everyone else around him sees. He never knows the mood of his region or his parish. So when he speaks, how far removed from reality are his words! how remote from him is the life of all those listening to him! And when he acts, how many of his actions are ill-timed!

There is a real danger that we priests may fail to see the drama of the century (if we may call it that), the struggle being waged right under our eyes each day, the anxious material struggle for their daily bread in which all our parishioners are engaged. We ourselves have almost no experience of permanent insecurity of this kind, of permanent uncertainty, or of the stern realities

---

[1] *Les grandes Écoles*—the various types of schools which prepare men and women for the professions. Admittance is by competitive examinations for which the lyceums prepare the students.

of life. But there is another struggle, perhaps even a more bitter one: the struggle between God and sin. Nor do we sufficiently see it as the tragedy it is. Somewhere in his book, *The Lord*, Guardini says that the Passion is not a tragedy, because we know that the words of eternal life are in it. That is true enough, but it is a truth that may mislead us: it ought to be a source of great confidence for us and a light in days of distress; but it is also a threat to us, since it can give leave to a dangerous kind of tranquillity to gain entrance into our souls.

The missionary is, of course, quite certain that the Christian cause will triumph in the end. He entertains no doubt about the outcome of the struggle. But he also knows that, even if the history of the Church and of the world is not a tragedy in the sense that evil has any chance of coming out on top, the history of each individual and of every society is a tragedy. He knows that in this tragedy he has a part to play, a crucial part. His every movement and his every decision may have terrible repercussions; tremendous issues may be decided by his industry or his indolence. And for this reason the missionary is alert to the history that is being made; he knows what is taking place; he passes judgment on it; he evaluates it.

It should trouble our consciences to see how we sometimes abuse the highest truths in order to justify our peace of mind and go on living in an unreal world. We know, for example, that God's actions count for more than ours and that He can get along without us; and so we come to the point where our blunders no longer upset us and our failures no longer set us looking for their cause. Again, our liturgy carefully preserves rites that are eloquent memorials of our Christian past. They were the products of a vital atmosphere which is time-less. But if we fail to replace them in such a living atmosphere, our contact with them is only too likely to make ritualists out of us, to accustom us in our everyday life to use words unconnected with reality and to hang on to methods totally ineffective in our world of today.

We want to make it clear that a real missionary will never delude himself with words and statistics and methods. In his parish he will not spend his time and consume his energy in trying to keep life in those activities which he knows have seen their day and are now incapable of having any influence. Perhaps a handful of people use them and thereby find a way of spending their leisure time. But he wants more than that. He has no time to lose in conserving museum pieces. When the intelligent shopkeeper inventories his stock or analyzes his sales, he does a thorough job of it; when the shrewd industrialist examines his income from the plant, he makes it a point to know the real returns from each shop and each workman. Neither one of them holds on to a useless annex, an unprofitable enterprise, or a piece of broken machinery. So it is with the true missionary.

He knows that the work is too much for him and that he cannot do it all. He therefore chooses the item which gives a good return, and in choosing he does his best to be uninfluenced by sentiment, snobbishness, or routine.

When we carefully examine the activities in which

priests are engaged, we are astounded to see how many useless things they continue to hang on to for no other reason than a kind of unconscious sentimentality. It is disconcerting to listen to two priests, two apostles, discussing new moves to be made or reforms to be introduced into their apostolate, whether the innovations concern church ceremonies or parish activities or Catholic Action. You can see at once that their decisions are based only on impressions pure and simple, and not at all on real situations which they have observed in the course of their own experience, or on the returns which they expect in view of such real situations. One will insist on the need for continuing one activity, while the other will lay down certain limits for his contemplated ventures; and neither of them has any compelling reasons based on figures or on real situations which he has closely scrutinized. Both, in fact, have nothing but vague motives dressed up as *rationes convenientiae—rationes*, however, that have nothing to do with reason.

In one parish everything is concentrated on a particular activity; in another a certain institution is stubbornly maintained at any cost. It takes everyone's time and energy and absorbs all the financial resources of the parish; but no one ever asks himself whether there might not be some better way, whether it might not be possible to accomplish a hundred times more by devoting more manpower and money to some other enterprise. In the meantime everything else is endangered, because all the waking hours of the pastor and all his energy is taken up by the one activity which, by habit or personal preference, he is resolved to maintain.

No missionary will be satisfied with a name or a plan. He will not think, for example, that all the children of his parish are being evangelized simply because he has a recreation center, nor will he continue the recreation center simply because he himself used to frequent one as a boy. He will not believe that the working class has been reached when each of his curates has a Jocist section under his wing. He will not imagine that the families in his parish are having the gospel preached to them because the Catholic Family Movement has been established. He knows only too well that recreation centers, Jocist sections, and Catholic family groups can all of them be sterile and lifeless things, nor is he tempted to feel that his work is done once he has begun to use a certain method or to follow out a certain directive. He always wants to know exactly where he is. Whenever a problem comes up, he asks himself once more the question Foch used to ask himself: "What is our objective?" Our objective is, not to have a Jocist section, but to evangelize the working class; not to have such and such an activity for the neighborhood children, but to see that Christianity plays its part in their lives.

When people see how certain parishes and institutions are run, they say to themselves that if an industrial concern or a business were run so it would have gone on the rocks long ago. Perhaps, unfortunately, that is just what has happened. It is painful to see that the children of light are not so wise in the affairs of the kingdom of

God as the children of darkness are in their own domain.

A true missionary realizes that God gives His grace to men for a purpose, to enable them to carry out His will; and he realizes that he himself is the instrument of that will. He is certain of final victory, and yet he knows that the winning of the victory depends in part on him. His vision embraces the whole world, and for that very reason he works in the concrete situation which has the dimensions of his parish, without separating his parish from the world. It is because he is a realist that he devotes himself just as much to the small everyday jobs as to the broad reforms that are required.

An Uneasy Man

We described the militant Communist as one who sees and does not reconcile himself to what he sees. This is a distinguishing trait of his. Many, in fact, see and countenance what they see; many who live surrounded by misery are resigned to it, shrugging it off with a "There is nothing we can do about it." The militant Communist is in a perpetual state of anger. Everything stirs him to revolt: the household where the wages are exhausted before the week is up; the accident at work which means destitution in the home; the brutality of a foreman. Everything feeds his revolutionary fever; everything intensifies his reaction: "There must be a change." He is forever contrasting the reality he meets along his path with the dream he bears within him. And the further he advances on the path, the more intense his passion becomes.

78

Transpose this to another plane, without putting the Communist altogether out of your mind, and you have the state of mind of the missionary. He is a man who is not on the side of evil and is not reconciled to it.

The reader may think this is self-evident. Perhaps. But I remember the pastor of a small parish whom I once met. He said to me, almost lightheartedly: "Everything is going to the dogs here, you know. For the twenty years that I have been here things have been constantly going downhill. But, after all, it will have to end some-day. When they reach the bottom, things will have to start up again." To him his parish seemed like a rubber ball. He was not uneasy. We grant, of course, that his is an extreme case; but how many priests are really uneasy? We do not mean with that timorous uneasiness which is always reckoning up catastrophes, for there are only too many of that type. We mean rather with the healthy uneasiness which keeps a man from going to sleep. The majority have grown used to the situation. They are well aware that four people out of five in their parish, and often less, never set foot in their church. But that is the way things are. Perhaps when they first arrived in the parish, they looked about with furrowed brows; but long ago the situation ceased to worry them. Every now and then you will hear a pastor say: "Little John, who made his first Communion the other day, has no faith, I am quite sure." The pastor himself had given him per-mission to make it. A few minutes' reflection would show that the whole passive crowd of people sitting in church for Mass is not receiving its spiritual nourishment and does not understand what is going on at all. But it is better not to think of these things too long. Where there is good will—and there is plenty of that—some routine practices will be revised under the pressure of a universal movement; there will, for example, be a few timid attempts at the dialogue Mass. But because there is no personal uneasiness behind the changes, the results are scanty; and perhaps such half failures even give rise to a certain satisfaction, enabling the priest to say, "I told you so." In any case, the routine drags on in essence: there is no deep disquiet; there is the same incapacity to receive a shock.

The true missionary is always receiving shocks. A scandal breaks out; a horrible example of ignorance comes to light; a home breaks up; a child is morally abandoned; a leader deserts the cause; a baptism is a mockery—anything like this affects him, because he is vulnerable to everything. "If they only knew," he says to himself, "such things would not happen. And if they do not know, they have not been taught. They do not know what love is. They should have been told. Is it not my fault?"

The true missionary has not lost the ability to be surprised or to become indignant. We are not thinking of the young priest fresh from the seminary and just discovering evil; it is natural that everything should surprise him, because he knew nothing of it before. We have in mind rather the missionary who has already been working a long time and has nothing more to learn, and yet is not blasé. He sees the same things occurring over and over again until they are familiar to him, but his priestly sensibilities are not blunted. Each fresh blow he receives only strengthens his conviction that there must be a change. It is no morbid love of novelty or inborn restlessness at the root of his uneasiness. It is the *caritas Christi urget nos;* it is the gospel, which is for him the ferment of perpetual renewal, the ferment of revolution. Have we not time and again in our lives said, *"Emitte Spiritum tuum . . . et renovabis faciem terrae"?* A renewal of the face of the world! The missionary is haunted by the thought of this renewal: it is a veritable passion with him. He is not afraid of it, as are so many others who, when confronted with reforms proposed to them or already under way, are always inclined to ask themselves where it is all going to end. He is too shocked by the wretchedness of the things that are, to consider their disappearance a loss. Hence, he is ready for any improvement and is ever on the lookout for something better. He projects his apostolic uneasiness on the whole world. That dechristianization is such a widespread phenomenon is a perpetual source of pain to him. It is a fact which he keeps before his eyes so that he may never forget it, and before his mind so that he may keep looking for a solution.

We have already mentioned an international meeting we recently attended. It was noticeable that the laymen of the eleven countries there represented had observed the same phenomenon. According to them, there was a serious condition of dechristianization (even—and, in fact, especially—in the reputedly Christian countries);

81

and, at the same time, a clergy unconcerned about and ignorant of the true state of affairs.

Every fact and every failing that comes to the missionary is armed with a question mark. He cannot see or hear anything without asking himself what bearing it has on the missionary problem. Perhaps it is a new film or a newspaper article, a new social or philanthropic venture; it makes no difference, because he always thinks immediately of the good or bad influence it will have on his cause. That consideration is the scale in which he weighs everything.

He is consequently able to go out and make contacts without waiting for others to come to him. He is not a functionary working at his job for so many hours and no more; he is a missionary all the time, and he never misses a chance to impart his enthusiasm to others. You may catch sight of him in a sacristy talking to a young man who happened to come along; and perhaps in another corner an old priest, one of those who have grown used to things as they are, may be saying to himself, "Look at him! He can't see a young fellow without falling all over him." The old man has unconsciously hit the nail on the head. The missionary "falls all over" every soul that comes within his range. And when he comes face to face with misery and misunderstanding and suffering in all its forms, he feels the enormous distance between the reality and the dream that he is carrying within him. With his whole being he wants to lessen that distance and is more than ever determined that there must be a change.

Does this surprise you? "To be at ease is to be un-safe" (Newman).

A Victim

In this battle, it is not the immediate results that count. As everybody knows, one of the leading themes of the Communist theory is that we have hardly begun to see the realization of integral communism. Several generations will have to be sacrificed before this objective is achieved. We will not see the results. We are working for a society that is still to come. The real Communist leader, the type who has not lost the fire of his Communist faith, the type found especially among the rank and file—he is filled with this spirit.

It is certainly sad to see so much generosity misdirected in the service of a cause which will never satisfy the hopes it arouses, since it considers only man, and man cut off from God. But it is impossible not to admire the inner inspiration, which is an unconscious transposition from the very essence of Christianity.

Sine sanguinis effusione non fit remissio. Without the Cross there is no redemption. The suffering Redeemer is on the program, and His provisional failure also. To human eyes the story of Christ is a failure, and His Passion a defeat. The harvest was to come afterwards, the never-ending harvest that was to crop up on the graves of the martyrs and of their brothers in sacrifice. Only with the eyes of faith do we know that the Cross is a victory; even after twenty centuries of history have strengthened our faith, we still need faith to see the

Cross as a confirmation of our faith. Even the greatest Apostle of all, St. Paul, on the day of his death had to look to his faith for assurance that his life had not been spent in vain. "One sows, another reaps." If a man wants to reap everything he sows, it will only be a small garden he can cultivate. If you wish to be a missionary, you have to renounce success; you have to welcome joyfully the words addressed to you: "May the kingdom of Christ move on over your body."

"He who would save his life will lose it, he who loses his life for my sake will gain it." This powerful proverb of Our Lord's, which is true in so many different ways, finds its most striking application in the apostolate. In the struggle which makes up the apostolate, victory goes to those who are willing to lose. Not to lose the battle (on the contrary, they are sure of winning it), but to lose themselves. Victory belongs to those who are willing to lay down their lives in the struggle without asking to see the victory. Ah! it is no doubt quite possible that they will sometimes speak like the Communist militant who dreamed of the renewal of the world: "I would certainly like to live long enough to see the beginning of the new world . . ." But this desire is only a manifestation of their optimism and their faith in their cause. In fact, they will never say this seriously, for they know that the kingdom is not of this world. At the same time, however, they know that the kingdom of God is already in the making in this world, that it is in the making every day, that they must work without respite for it, that the victory is already won, but that they are the ones who must enable the multitude to benefit by it. *Adveniat regnum tuum!* It is coming even now; it is coming invisibly into every soul which allows itself to be won over by Love. It sometimes shows its face when a group or a parish gives proof of fraternity or devotion. But then you can be sure that the Cross is in the background. The kingdom of God does not come through a successful meeting from which the cry goes up, "Hail to Christ the King!" It does not come through a victory at the polls. It does not come through perfectly organized parish societies, nor even through magnificent ceremonies. All these things have their importance, greater or less as the case may be; but we must not let ourselves take them for the real thing, or mistake these successes for the victory of Christ. *Haec est victoria fides nostra.* There is no victory for Christ except where there is an increase of faith or of love.

This is the same distinction we made in *Revolution in a City Parish* and which seems to us of prime importance —the distinction between God's kingdom and ours. The missionary refuses to seek his own kingdom. He is even uneasy when he sees the beginning of a little kingdom of his own: *Non nobis, Domine, non nobis, sed nomini tuo da gloriam.* He has eyes for nothing but the kingdom of God, the kingdom which comes interiorly and which uses as its instruments all those who are willing to lose their life with Christ. And this it is which, in the final analysis, explains why he is never discouraged. When a man looks for immediate results it is quite natural that he should be easily discouraged, just as it is quite natural

85

that he should react to failure by pseudo-spiritual submission which inclines him to give up trying to accomplish anything. The missionary does not "resign" himself
to failure. He gives himself through his failure, because
he sees it as a kind of condition of the final victory. He
adds his own failure to the great stream that is sweeping
on to ultimate triumph. He knows he is a victim, and
that is what he wants to be.

VISION OF THE CHURCH

A world vision such as we have just sketched will give
us a missionary and even a Christian missionary, but not
necessarily a Catholic missionary.

A man can be a Catholic missionary only if his name
is written in a Catholic context. This Catholic context is
the Church. To be a Catholic missionary is to belong to
the Church. The vision of what the Church is and of
what membership in the Church entails will determine
the missionary's whole outlook and behavior, the whole
tenor of his conduct and life.

The word "mission" evokes the idea of being sent. No
one sends himself. A mission is something one receives.
"As my Father has sent me, I also send you." We receive
a mission from Christ, from Christ living in His Church,
to which He has committed the duty of preparing the
coming of His kingdom.

There was a time when the word "mission" was used
exclusively of apostolic expeditions which went beyond
the frontiers of Christendom. But that was an age in
which there was a Christendom. The word continued to

be used thus long after there had ceased to be a Christendom (though many were still under the illusion that it continued to exist).

Today paganism is everywhere. There is now no longer any danger of confusing the kingdom of Christ with the kingdom of St. Louis or even with the Holy Roman Empire. Is this something to be regretted? The invasion of paganism certainly is. But it is all to the good that the mask has been torn away from it and that it now appears in the open instead of veiling its face. In any event, the Church has profited by this development to the extent that she is again, as in the Apostolic age, able to see herself as a ferment, as a leaven spread wherever the dough of humanity needs to rise. The mission today is *ad intra*. It is here in France, in Italy, in Spain, in South America, in the United States. It is in your own parish, even if your parish happens to be one of the so-called "Catholic" ones. The entire Church is in a state of mission.

That the Church is in a state of mission in a dechristianized parish is only too evident; but it is also in the same state in the "practicing" parish. This is true because, first of all, only rarely does the practice of the practicing parish run as high as fifty per cent, and no parish can forget the half of its members that are still to be won. It is true also because practicing Catholics, as well as others, are the object of a mission, the purpose of which is to make the charity of Christ take root in them. Finally, and above all, it is true because the rest of the Church needs the mission, and no Christian community

87

can be without solicitude for the rest of the body. No community, whether a parish or a religious community, can call itself Christian if it isolates itself and does not participate in the perpetual mission of the whole Church. All who really possess the spirit of the Church are animated by a missionary spirit, even if their environment is entirely Catholic.

This applies to every member of the community, to priest and layman alike—to the layman every bit as much as to the priest, since the layman too has received a mission from the hierarchy. It is not a matter of choice; it is bound up with one's status as a member of the community, for the community itself is a portion of the Church.

The reader may think we are laboring the obvious. It is true enough that all this has been said already and repeated countless times. But when you see the spirit which exists in so many of our "good parishes," you feel duty-bound to say it again. Those who are, or think they are, the *beati possidentes*, seem to look upon missionary problems as no concern of theirs. Even when you try to interest them in something vital to almost the whole Church, they do not hesitate to say that it does not concern them at all. "That does not concern us." What a small concept of "us" that implies! They have no qualms about planning their activities without giving a thought to the possibility of co-ordinating them with the work in other parts. This means a loss to the whole missionary movement and a loss to them as well. For they are thereby losing that dynamism which, before long, they will need more than they think; perhaps they already need it for the reconquest of what, without their knowing it, is now being lost to them.

We would even go so far as to say that these almost wholly Catholic parishes are the ones which ought to be the most missionary. And we see at least two reasons why this should be so.

In the first place, they are Christian and therefore fully equipped to do Christ's work, to abide by the dictates of the Church, and to receive a "mission." Well and good. Now let us see how a political party, for example, wages an election campaign. What would we think of a party which, at election time, paid no attention at all to those districts where it has a majority, making no campaign there, and fighting only in those districts where it is certain to be defeated? The party must, of course, even without hope of immediate success, put up a fight in those localities where it is unknown or in the minority; but it must also work where its chances of success are good, and make sure of the victory which is within its reach. Or, again, take a businessman. Will you ever see him leave a market where business is good and go to one where there are no customers? Pardon these comparisons: they are not much to our liking either, but they illustrate our point well enough. It is obviously necessary to go after the one lost sheep. This we have said so often that our attitude ought to be known. But at the same time we also have to look for ways to enlighten the sheep that are beginning to wander off and look for the roads which lead to them. And surely it is easier to inject the missionary spirit into a parish where there is good will and where everyone has the faith and is ready to heed the directives of the Church. Do we really appreciate what an increase in power would result, particularly for the Church in France, if all the Catholic regions were to acquire a real sense of their missionary obligation and act according to it? Is it not strange that certain dioceses with an ample number of priests find it so hard to part with vocations for the Mission of France or for religious congregations, although in the past it was these very dioceses which were the principal providers of vocations for the missions in China and Africa?

In the second place, the mission means, not propaganda, but testimony; and it functions much like the light on the bushel. What we need is to show the world real Christian living. The great need is to plant "witnesses" of Christ in society, community witnesses as well as individual ones. Imagine what a testimony to the truth it would be for the whole of France if our practicing parishes were truly Christian communities in which rectitude, justice, and charity were genuine everyday realities. What a testimony to the truth if we could say to our dechristianized populations: "You want to know what Christianity is and what happiness it can bring into the world? Go to the Vendée, to Britanny, to Anjou, and see for yourself what life is like there, how the priests there act, and how the Catholics there live!" We are not asking for universal sanctity; still, we cannot help but think of the wonderful spectacle it might have been for the whole of France if there had been one province to which we could have pointed and said: "See that Catholic region! There is no black market there!"

The missionary spirit is a spirit of the Church; the spirit of the Church is a missionary spirit.

The missionary keeps his eyes fixed on this vision of the Church in the world: a Church on the march, a Church in the minority, a Church misunderstood, opposed and ignored.

He is interested in what happens to the Church, and not only in what is happening in his parish, his activity or his movement. He thinks according to the dimensions of the universe. And what excuse could there be for thinking otherwise in our world? Every day, the newspapers and the radio bring us face to face with world problems and make us see how the whole world is affected by events which occur anywhere on the face of the globe.

The missionary thinks this way and, because he does, he also realizes that he is a man of the Church, that his actions constitute a commitment for the Church, that he represents her, that he is responsible for her, that he either helps her to advance or handicaps her. This is true of every priest, and indeed of every Catholic layman as well—at least of everyone known as such. Whether we like it or not, whether we find it a nuisance or not, this is a fact, and a fact none of us can ever afford to forget: my attitude, my words, my smile or my forbidding appearance, the way I offer my hand, the way I judge, the way I administer the sacraments and the way I enter into the Mass—this and everything else I do results in a favorable or unfavorable judgment being formed of the Church of Jesus Christ.

It must not be imagined that the missionary feels like patting himself on the back when he hears someone say: "You, sure, you're all right. You aren't the same kind of priest as the others; but why aren't the others like that?" He has no desire to be an exception. Far from it. But such a remark surprises him, because he is convinced that he is doing only the most elementary things. On the other hand, it is a pity that anyone should have to admit such a remark is true. Unfortunately, it is true. When an individual Catholic or an individual priest is a real witness, that is a good thing. When a group or a parish community gives witness, that is even better. Our witnessing, however, will be as effective as it should be only when it is the mass that witnesses: Christians and priests as a whole, our parishes as a whole. It will, in fact, be effective witnessing when it is the witnessing of the Church, or at least (since we are writing in French) of the Church of France. Love for the Church should make it impossible for any Catholic leader or any member of the clergy to isolate himself from the missionary movement.

The fact that we are making commitments for the Church forces us to think twice before making any move or taking any step, but it also serves as a stimulus to us and an invitation to go forward. It makes us realize that we are not marching alone. When we ourselves have to bear painful opposition and incomprehension from those around us, it helps to know that in other places, and in more places all the time, the missionary movement is going ahead. Furthermore, it helps to know that this missionary movement is essential to the Church, and that we are in the right, as against every form of stagnation and routine.

Thus, to the missionary it is of the utmost importance to see that his work is carried out in union with the whole Church. He does not take to the road alone or set out to do battle alone. The ground he covers is put down as part of the whole forward movement of the advancing Church. He will therefore be careful to keep in contact with the Church—a need which entails many obligations.

His first obligation is to keep his leaders informed. Our leaders make no claim to be like the heroes of Molière's comedy: "We, men of quality as we are, know everything without ever having learned anything." Our leaders know quite well that there is no one more isolated than a superior whose subjects, in an attempt to please him, tax their ingenuity to draw a rose-colored curtain of pious optimism between him and reality. Our leaders are more like Foch when he said to a liaison officer: "Do not tell me what you think will please me, tell me what is true." They have the assistance of grace and of the Holy Spirit, but they need to be kept informed. And they can be kept informed only by the priests and laymen who are in actual contact with the great masses of the people, believers and unbelievers. The Vatican and the diocesan chancery are like ourselves: they can work no more than fifteen or sixteen hours a day, and in this time they cannot acquire a personal knowledge of everything. The Pope sees only what is brought to his attention. The bishops hear only what they are told. It is the missionary's duty to give them an exact picture of the temper of the times as he knows it, of the needs of his people, of the precise degree of their ignorance, and the reason for it as he sees these things. It is his duty also to let them know what the people are thinking and saying; to tell them the story of his own experiences, what he hoped to accomplish and how far he has succeeded; and to suggest possible remedies for particular situations.

Sometimes we hear bitter remarks about the failure of superiors to understand the real situation. Do those who make such remarks do anything to clear away the misconceptions of their superiors? Have bishops been able to get a clear picture of the true state of affairs from some of the reports that are made at the time of the pastoral visitation or from the accounts that appear in the religious bulletin of the parish? Whose fault is it that bishops are sometimes poorly informed? Who put them on the wrong track? We all know that it requires a certain amount of courage to tell the truth, much more courage than to describe conditions in a way that will be pleasing and flattering. If we lack this courage which our leaders expect us to have, we are not the kind of missionaries we should be.

There is also the matter of loyalty, the loyalty we owe our superiors and the loyalty we owe those under us. Every minor superior, indeed every man who is entrusted with even the smallest responsibility, is an intermediary between the one who gave him his mission and those to whom he is sent. The priest as an intermediary has this responsibility to a greater degree than others. By his very nature, he is the bridge that joins men to God, and the faithful to the hierarchy of the Church. He is not only the representative of the hierarchy before the faithful; he is also the representative of the faithful before the hierarchy. He is the pastor of the faithful; their souls have been placed in his care; and it is his duty to see that his leaders know the sufferings and the needs of his people. Often enough, the faithful, especially if they are ordinary people, will experience needs and sufferings and difficulties without knowing how to formulate them or without daring to express them, at least to those in high places. Perhaps the idea of making them known to their leaders will never even occur to them, or, if it does, they will lack the courage; and sometimes they will be unable to express their sentiments even to themselves. Who will be their spokesmen, if not we, their pastors? When we see and hear things and keep them to ourselves, when we come face to face with problems every day and lack the courage to make them known to those above us, whose responsibility for these masses is greater than our own, we are at one and the same time betraying our leaders and our sheep.

The missionary has another obligation which is even harder to live up to: adjusting his pace to that of the Church. All agree that we are supposed to lead. The Church counts on us to go ahead, and so we have at times to assume responsibilities which not everyone can assume. But at the same time we have to remember that we are part of a great fighting body, one which is not only spread out over today's battlefield but which also extends far back into history, one which has its traditions and is conditioned by its past. The term "vanguard" (*avant-garde*) is one that most of us are very tired of hearing used for everything and for nothing— to designate, for example, those who are experimenting with audacious methods as well as those who are only restoring things that should never have been allowed to disappear (and who are, in fact, only the vanguard of the rear guard). But since people insist on calling us the vanguard, we will not make a fuss about it. In any case, if we are the vanguard, we will have to keep in mind that the vanguard has no right to cut itself off from its bases and set out in search of adventure. Should it do so, it would be putting itself in danger of being wiped out and would be deserting the main body of the troops. Let us drop the metaphor. Only at the price of exposing the faithful to bewilderment and of bringing on divisions and regrettable reactions can any one of us, no matter who he is, launch any innovation, unless it has been approved by higher authority. We must, of course, be clear about what constitutes a dangerous innovation, and not call such those things which ought to be the rule for every pastor who is really concerned for the welfare of his flock. An explanation of the ceremonies at a funeral or a translation of the prayers, to take an example from the domain of liturgy, is not a dangerous innovation. But there are other innovations for which there is no real need: the creation of new forms of Catholic Action movements, the holding of inopportune meetings which may interfere with an action of the whole hierarchy, the celebration of Mass in the vernacular by a priest in public, and so on. The common good of the Church is at stake in every new step we take. We may never take such a step without considering its effects on the common good and its repercussions on the community as a whole; and, if it is an important step, we must first propose it to the authority responsible for the common good.

In the parish community itself the same holds good. Here also there must be no reckless pushing ahead heedlessly of the main body of troops. It is the simplest thing in the world to start a missionary movement into which a small number, those most easily led, will enter enthusiastically. But what good does it do to record an advance of this kind when no one else follows? It is the whole parish that ought to be missionary, not merely the few; the whole parish has to be a missionary unit in its liturgy, its teaching, its activities. Some will, of course, be more dynamic than others, and it is they who will have to set the pace. But a man who is supposed to set the pace is of no use to his companions when he streaks off several miles ahead of them. He must never lose contact with them.

The transformations and advances of the parish must affect all the parishioners; and therefore, to achieve more universal results, we will at times have to slow down our pace. Suppose, for example, I want to have my people sing. It would be relatively easy to form a *schola cantorum* of twenty young ladies; everyone would be happy; after a year or two, such a choir would be quite creditable. But no one else would have the courage to join in with it. If you think you need a *schola cantorum* to guide the rest, you must, at the same time you form it, do all in your power to get everyone to sing. It is the same with the Jocist section which gets off to such a brilliant start that it soon leaves the mass of young workers far behind. Perhaps a word of warning is in order here. We can already see some of our readers seizing upon these words of ours, convinced that they justify stagnation and getting ready to sing once more their favorite refrain: "Let us not go too fast." Before they settle back in their comfortable chairs, let us make it clear that, just because it is much harder to get a whole parish moving than a select group, we must set about it at once and keep at it all the time.

This same solicitude for the Church calls for the teamwork about which we shall have more to say later. Since all of us (we priests and our lay people with us) belong to the Church, we cannot work in isolation at parallel tasks; we are yoked together to do the same work, and that work is the work of the Church.

For the same reason, we shall do our best to adjust our pace to that of the neighboring parishes, the national organizations of Catholic Action, and the religious Orders. The Church militant is a collaboration on a grand scale in the service of the same Leader; this means that there will be different tasks to be carried out, but that all will be directed to the one end under the inspiration of the same Spirit, the Spirit of Love.

Certain parishes, certain groups, certain individual missionaries will perhaps be called upon to bear witness in a distinctive way and to blaze trails. They will be "on a special mission," so to speak, and will serve as a leaven for the rest; but they must not forget that they belong to the Church and that they have an obligation to serve the community as a whole.

This is the kind of missionary spirit that has always been proper to the Church. Every time the Church has allowed it to take a concrete form, she has had to take a risk. There is a risk involved today as there was in the past, but there is no added reason to fear the risk. The Church sent her missionaries, as she is still sending them, to far off lands. She was not unaware of the risks involved: the risks to their bodies, because of the climate and the hostility of the people; and the risks to their souls also, because isolation can bring on discouragement and because there were other temptations to which they would be exposed. Still, she did not hesitate to send them.

When today the Church sends her missionaries into factories, she is not unaware of the dangers of another kind which lie in wait for them; but, all things considered, there is no more reason to worry over the priest you send into the factory than over the one you send into tropical regions where he is surrounded by people of loose moral standards. The Church's inclination to expand has always enabled her to overcome such fears and put to one side the motives that would bid her lie still.

We must, however, hold firmly to two principles. The first: the more advanced the post you are holding, the more necessary it is that you should have been given it by lawful authority; the individual ought not to choose his role in the Church, and least of all when there is danger of bringing discredit on her. The second: the more advanced the position the missionary holds, the more necessary it is for him to be in communication with the center of the Church, with a community, and with his bishop.

When he is thus linked to the Church, through his mandate and his fidelity, the missionary will be certain that he is doing God's work and that he is accomplishing something worth-while for God's kingdom.

VISION OF THE LOVE OF CHRIST

But the missionary spirit will be a truly Christian spirit only if its consuming and overpowering motive is that of making the Person of Christ known and loved and served. We are, of course, heralds of a Church; but not of a Church as an organization, nor a Church that stands for order above all else, nor yet a Church that is primarily a temporal institution. It is the Church of Christ that we preach, the Church that is the society of God's children gathered together in Christ, the Church that is the Body of Christ. We preach the Truth, but not a theory or a Christian philosophy or even a theology; the Truth we preach is the Word of God, the Word made flesh: "I am the Truth, I who speak to you." We announce the gospel teaching, but not only the message (as we might if we were in the Old Testament): it is the Messenger Himself that we announce.

Since Harnack's time some have been more or less inclined to say that charity is "the essence of Christianity." It is not so. The essence of Christianity is a living Person; the essence of Christianity is Christ. It is not a moral system, however lofty and beautiful, that we have to proclaim. We proclaim Christ, the Incarnation of a God who is love. The worship we offer is Christ: Christ praying and Christ offering Himself through our hearts and voices and hands. And the cause for which we want victory is the cause of the Person of Christ; we want to see Christ known to all, in order that all may love Him.

The priest becomes a real missionary only on the day that the vision of Christ as center of the world's history takes hold of him, the day that he begins to see Christ as the One who gathers together the scattered children of God, as the human manifestation of the Father's love for men, as the crown of all creation, as the adorer of the Father, as the choirmaster of humanity's adoration, as priest, and as victim. On that day, he stops preaching theses which leave most men cold, and he begins to reveal the moving mystery of the God who so loved men that He gave them His only Son.

The missionary is not an exegete, a controversialist or a philosopher; he is the herald of a fact. He proclaims that God became man and dwelt in our midst. He holds up the Cross and tells men what it means. He recounts the story of Jesus, how the prophecies and events of the Old Testament prepared the way for Him, how He lived here on earth, suffered and died, rose again and ascended into heaven. He declares that Christ is present in the Church and in the Eucharist. He announces that Christ is to come back again, and that we are on our way to meet Him. A discussion may leave us neutral; but a man—we take sides for or against him. The missionary announces the Man-God and invites men to declare themselves.

The men of our age, in spite of all their protestations against dictators and dictatorships, are quite ready to allow themselves to be guided and led by a man. The contradiction is only an apparent one. They are looking for a great leader whom it is safe to follow, a leader they can admire and obey—above all, a leader they can love. The missionary's work is surely made easier by this characteristic aspiration of our times. It is, in fact, quite easy to point to Christ as the true leader, the One who did not come to enslave others but to serve them, the only one who does not make use of others but gives Himself for them. But it is easy only if people can see that we are sincere, and only as long as they do not spy the ghost of clericalism lurking behind the Cross of Christ the King.

There is one more point. If you wish to make a leader loved, you must love him yourself, love him passionately. But first of all you must know him intimately. When a man can say of a great human leader, "I know him: I have seen him," everyone who trusts the speaker is reduced to silence. We must therefore have a personal knowledge of Christ, a knowledge which is not bookish or speculative or affected. We acquire it through a loving familiarity with Holy Scripture and with the Gospels in particular. We acquire it also through prayer and through the Mass, in the very heart of our prayer and of the Mass, filled as it is with the Scriptures and the Gospels illuminated by the unique light of the Paschal mystery which we are celebrating and commemorating as we offer Christ in person.

As far as the missionary himself is concerned, there is no substitute for a close contact with the Bible. The missionary is by his very nature a bearer of the Good News, and he must speak in the name of a Person whom he has some experience of hearing and seeing.

There is for us, therefore, a distinct method of studying the Bible. If we have a complaint to make against our seminary professors, it is that they did not teach us to read the Bible and to look in it for the one and only Christ. They taught us exegesis, but did not teach us to look at the Psalms, the Prophets, the Gospels, and St. Paul with the fresh and keen and mobile eyes a man needs when he is looking for the countenance and the thoughts of Jesus Christ our Lord, for His intentions and His love. We know a seminarian who was severely reprimanded because he tried to construct from the Gospels a picture of Christ's appearance and character. He was accused of "naturalism." It is still more painful to recall the stricture of a Catholic, strongly tempted to turn to Protestantism, who said to us, "In Protestant churches they speak of nothing but Jesus; in Catholic pulpits they speak of nothing but moral conduct." This is, of course, an exaggeration; but, if our lips are to speak out of the abundance of our hearts, we must become familiar with Jesus Christ in our studies and meditations and prayers. We will never succeed unless our spirituality is more than a mere "moral" spirituality, unless it is a meeting with Christ and an unaffected intimacy with Him.

Strictly speaking, there is no such thing as a missionary spirituality. Men live and teach many spiritualities, among which none is especially indicated for the missionary, just as none is forbidden him. Yet it is true that the missionary needs to live in a close and personal union with Christ, and that his need is greater than that of any other Christian. "For I determined to know nothing among you except Jesus Christ, and him crucified."

V

Some Materials for a Missionary Spirituality

Spirituality is a big word, and we want it to be clear from the outset that we are using the word only because it is the best one we can think of. The various forms of spirituality were never so much discussed as in our day. The traditional spirituality has been confronted with the modern spirituality; comparisons have been made between the various forms: Benedictine, Franciscan, Dominican, etc. Some have advocated a spirituality for the laity; some have attempted to define a spirituality for the priest; and some have even questioned the very existence of these various spiritualities.

It is not our purpose in this chapter to have our say about such controverted matters. When we speak of a missionary spirituality, we have no intention of comparing it with any other kind; and the idea of introducing a new spirituality is even further from our thoughts. Our purpose is much more modest. Convinced as we are that there must be a variety of the interior life which is characteristic of the missionary, we are simply asking ourselves what it is. It is to this characteristic variation of the interior life that we give the name "spirituality." Now we can let the authorities proceed with their disputes about the term.

The reader will not, therefore, expect to find here a treatise on spirituality, or even some elements of such a treatise. We have nothing to offer him in the way of theories worked out at a desk. We are simply taking a position from which we can observe a reality—a reality made up of the mission work to be done, the priests called upon to do it, their failures and their successes in the domain of the interior life, and our own experiences as well. When we observe this complex reality, we feel that we have something to say, that we have a word of advice to help our younger brethren avoid mistakes and find what we are searching for along with them.

"MISSIONARY"?

Often enough—much too often, in fact—has it been our experience to hear laymen or fellow priests calmly bestowing on us or on themselves the title "missionary," but it has never failed to set our nerves on edge. To their way of thinking, it is to be taken for granted that the Christian world can be divided into two parts or, so to speak, into two states: the static state and the missionary state. You make your choice between the two according to your tastes, or you are definitively assigned to one or the other by a mandate of the hierarchy.

But "missionary" is not a title one should be quick either to assume or to bestow.

And when you "are a missionary," you are not therefore entrenched in a definitive state or situation. You are a missionary to the extent you are a saint. You tend to become a missionary as you tend to become a saint. The missionary state is an ideal of the priestly life which Christ places before our eyes. To call oneself a missionary is as ridiculous as to call oneself a saint. It is nothing we can lay claim to, but only something we can tend to.

There is an effort to be made, a constant advance to be achieved, an ideal to be realized. All of these—the making of the effort, the achievement of the advance, the realization of the ideal—must spring from love and must develop our love. And precisely for this reason there is room for us to look for a spirituality in the full development of our being as missionaries.

To be a saint, to be a missionary—for us, these two are the same thing. For two reasons. The first is that, the present state of the Church and the world being what it is, it seems to us impossible that a priest once engaged in the apostolic ministry should find any other way of sanctifying himself than by becoming more and more missionary, by spending himself completely in the immense work to be done, and by forgetting himself that the work may be done through him. The second reason is that the man who wishes to mount towards God can find in his missionary zeal everything he needs in the way of genuine mortification. We explained this point in *Revolution in a City Parish*.

107

The Church has in the past found room for many other types of sanctity, and she will do so in the future. Yet it seems to us unlikely that even the contemplative can grow to his full stature in the love of God unless he too catches a touch of the "missionary fever." In any case, the sanctity of a priest appointed by his bishop to any kind of post in parish work must be a missionary sanctity. The demands of the work to be done impose on him the form of sanctity which God expects of him. The struggle for perfection and the missionary effort are not two parallel entities: they are so intimately intertwined that they are but one thing.

It might be a good thing to try inverting the terms of an expression we frequently use. We are often told: "Be holy, and you will surely be a good priest or a good missionary." Would it not be more correct to say: "Be a real priest or a real missionary, and in the effort to become one you will become a saint"? Sanctity does not pre-exist as a reality from which missionary work might come forth as a fruit. The fact is rather that, in our search for the fullness of the missionary spirit, we are enabled to discover the sanctity that is ours.

MORTIFICATION THROUGH THE MINISTRY OR THROUGH SPIRITUAL EXERCISES?

We all know that spiritual writers traditionally divide the spiritual life into the three ways: the purgative, the illuminative, and the unitive — or mortification, the practice of the virtues, and union with God. All the saints tell us, by their example as well as by their words,

108

that mortification is absolutely necessary for anyone who wishes to strive after perfection.

Could it not be that the time-honored mortifications, as we find them described in devotional books, have proved so discouraging to some people in our day that they have come to slight the very notion of mortification, considering it either impossible or unnecessary? "Times have changed." "Our health cannot stand up under that sort of thing." "We have too much work to do." Lay people say, "To work is to pray"; and priests, "A man can find God in his ministry."

Besides, is there still a place in the apostolic life of today for the "spiritual exercises" as they were taught us in the seminary? Would it not be advantageous to replace them by contact with souls and by the discovery of God which we make at every moment we are giving Him to souls? If it is true that the more missionary we become the closer we approach to sanctity, is it not enough to give oneself once for all without so much concern about the rest?

As the statement we made might, in fact, give rise to an illusion, we must dispel that illusion immediately. The fact that a man thinks he is a missionary does not mean he is on the road to sanctity. Let us repeat what we said before: it makes no more sense to call oneself a missionary than to call oneself a saint. The missionary state is a thing to which we tend. It consists in an unceasing effort, and this is like every other effort in that it needs a stimulus and a discipline. Its rhythm is that of two steps ahead and one back, with periods of weariness following on periods of generosity. There never comes a time when one can give up working on oneself.

The story of this struggle may be the story of a man's holiness. It may be possible to outline broadly a missionary spirituality after we have reached some firm conclusions based on many kinds of missionary experience. But we have no intention of doing that here. It is only as friends and brothers that we wish to speak, as friends and brothers who may enable others to see some things in a new light and who are glad of the chance to mention some of their own misgivings.

Some of our fellow priests are, to judge by their words, laboring under a serious misconception in the matter of holiness, a misconception which might seriously detract from their effectiveness as apostles.

It is clear that every type of spirituality aims at putting the soul in contact with God. It is equally clear that we can find God present in those around us and that our ministry affords us many opportunities to discover in souls the work of God—or God in person. How often have we not left the confessional, deeply moved by the confession someone has just made or by the resolute purpose of amendment manifested! How often, in the course of our priestly lives, have we not felt forced to overcome ourselves, to check up on ourselves spiritually, by our very struggle to rescue a young man from his bad habits or to save a home from shipwreck! And our own experience of administering the sacraments, of preaching and of time spent meeting people in the sacristy or rectory, all has proved to our satisfaction that these too can be excellent means of sanctification.

We would even go so far as to say that the ministry in itself presents continual opportunities for mortification, and that it is a grave defect in the training of seminarians that they are hardly taught to look for mortification in the exercise of their future ministry. In *Revolution in a City Parish* we did not spare our praises of this properly missionary asceticism—an adapted asceticism, granted, but one no less crucifying than our time-honored ascetical practices. It comes into play in the close watch we have to keep on our various apostolic movements; in the painful submission we must make to the demands of God's work; in the insistent demands charity makes on us, giving us no rest, refusing us any interior rest or feeling of satisfaction. *Sacerdoce oblige.* The priesthood has its obligations, and at times we have to pay an enormous price to live up to them. They may take us as far as the mortifications of the Curé of Ars, who immolated himself for his parish; but in ordinary everyday life they will regularly take the form of tiresome work, humble acceptance of reverses, abandonment of our own ideas for the good of the common work, surrender of things dear to us, and renouncement of our comfort and our habits.

It is a mortification not to choose one's work in a parish, but to take on any work at all according to the need.

It is a mortification for a priest to be confined to the confessional during an entire afternoon and be prevented from spending his time on the direction of a promising individual. Such direction has its place, no doubt; but the long wait in the confessional also has a place, and a more important one.

It is a mortification to learn how to listen to those who consult us, to see their problems as realities, suppressing our exasperation and smashing the shell of our indifference, which is the offspring of our self-love.

It is a mortification to keep our good humor when we have to deal with unreasonable people, if we do it because we know that every contact with a priest should leave a visitor with the memory of a door opened to the charity of Christ.

It is a mortification to take criticism to heart instead of turning up one's nose at it; it is the way we can learn what there is in us that grates on others and interferes with our service of them.

It is a mortification to be forever anxious to do better, and therefore to be always asking people (especially our own parishioners) for their opinion, in order to make adjustments and improvements and to give greater service.

It is a mortification not to linger with those who are fond of us, in order to keep our hearts and our time at the service of all. It is not an easy thing and it requires a detachment which hurts. Our fatigue, our isolation, and the affectionate solicitude of our friends are all leagued together against us, inviting us to let ourselves be surrounded and monopolized. Soon, we would no longer be "all things to all men." We must know the secret of tearing ourselves loose.

It is a mortification to be conscientious about the preparation of our sermons, our catechism classes, and the talks we have to give to groups, instead of indolently trusting to our glibness. This is a very trying mortification when our days are fully occupied and it seems to us that we could get by with a lesser effort.

It is a mortification to force ourselves to prepare carefully for, and to celebrate reverently, the sacraments of baptism and matrimony, funerals and the parish Mass, without ever doing anything negligently, without ever rushing through anything, being always careful to use the tone of voice and to give the explanations which will remind all that they are coming in contact with God. And it is especially a mortification to do this when we would prefer to be using our time otherwise (in visiting our district, for example), and to do it when only a few people attend—none of them leaders. But we must do it because we are at the service of the parish and because our brother priests will have to do what we refuse to do.

It is a mortification, and in no way an outmoded one, to be punctual in celebrating Mass and other ceremonies. We owe it to the faithful to be on time. There comes to my mind the case of a teacher in an Alpine village: on weekdays she used to walk several miles to assist at an early Mass, and sometimes after an hour's wait she had to leave without hearing Mass because the priest was not ready. Fortunately, this is an extreme instance; but there are others which, if not so extreme, are greatly to be regretted.

This effort to be punctual, as all the other things we have just mentioned, constitutes an "exercise," an *ascesis* in the fullest sense of the word. It is not the *ascesis* of the monk, but it is the one that our vocation of priest and missionary requires of us. Will anyone maintain that it is not as purifying, and sometimes as crucifying, as any other form of asceticism?

We recorded our views on this point in our earlier book, but we felt it necessary to repeat them here. Otherwise, what follows might lead the reader to think we had changed our mind.

There is need, in fact, to sound a warning. We must beware of concluding—on the pretext that the ministry, the apostolate, and priestly work are sanctifying activities—that we have done everything once we have given ourselves to these activities. The temptation to do so may be very strong. It is quite right, for example, to say that to find God all we need to do is carry out our ministry perfectly, our entire ministry as priests and missionaries. But are we sure that we are carrying it out perfectly? Carrying it out with the right spirit? Are we absolutely certain that we are not rather seeking ourselves and our own satisfaction in it? That we are not following our own impulses rather than the will of God? Are we certain that we are doing our work from motives that are sufficiently supernatural and disinterested? It is the quality of our work that is at stake, and it is in relation

114

to quality that the matter of the other means of sanctification has to be considered.

Certain means of sanctification were proposed to us in the seminary—meditation, spiritual exercises, spiritual direction; but they sometimes prove very difficult to keep up in a life engrossed in the thousand and one parochial activities. Fatigue and nervous exhaustion are always there threatening to render meaningless the moments set aside for prayer. These means of sanctification were presented to us so solemnly, as bastions to be held at any cost, almost as if they were the essential element in the priestly life; and here we find ourselves with duties so pressing that we can no longer see any way of being faithful to the exercises, or at least to the letter of them. In a word, we do not know what to make of it all.

Then there is this. At the very outset of our priestly lives everything is so new to us that it captivates us, and our first contacts with souls are extremely rewarding and very apt to rouse in us an immediate response of generosity and thanksgiving. The young priest, overflowing with his seminary meditations and with the fervor of a neophyte, experiences no difficulty in having a motive of charity in every word and every action.

Everything goes so well with him that, almost before he knows it, he finds himself tempted to say: "What good are all these bothersome exercises when the ministry itself provides me with everything I need in order to find God? There is no need for me to seek Him by means of formulas which have their value for seminarians, nor in definite times of meditation. I am meeting Him everywhere, all day long, in the people I am meeting and in the work I am doing."

Where does the fallacy lie? To us it seems to lie in mistaking the starting point for the goal. We would be glad of the chance to tell others that they hold up the traditional exercises to us as ends, whereas they are only means; but do not we ourselves too quickly believe that we are beginning to catch sight of the end, although we are neglecting the means?

"I have no need of anything but souls to find God." Very well indeed, brother priest of mine! But suppose a young Benedictine or Trappist novice declared to his Father Director: "Father, I want to know nothing but the unitive way. I am finding God in my prayer. The road you point out to me, which is the one the others are taking, with its controls and ascetical practices and counsels, is too long for me. I am taking a short cut." What would you say of him?

The contemplative has the obligation to *seek* God in his prayer. Freed as he is from other concerns, he spends his whole life long seeking God directly; but he seeks Him, and (as everyone knows) he can be the victim of many an illusion. What sensible spiritual director does not smile when he hears the declarations of certain splendid souls who think they have arrived at the highest forms of the mystical life? Those around them would have no difficulty reminding them of the most elementary laws of industry, considerateness, and patience.

Some Materials for a Missionary Spirituality

Are you not making the same mistake, brother priest? You claim to be finding God directly in souls. This should certainly be your aim. It is the perfection of your holiness. The contemplative must reach God through his whole life of prayer, and you must reach Him through your ministry. In the final analysis, both of us have to be contemplatives: to see God in souls is a kind of contemplation, and to serve Him through activity is perpetual adoration. But to both of us, to the monk as well as to myself, God is invisible and difficult of access; He desires to be sought after, and at times it is along dark roads that He wants us—groping and sometimes falling—to seek Him. If a man is to do this, he must have training, and this entails "exercises"; above all, he must go to the sources, where alone it is possible to drink in the light and strength of the Spirit. Otherwise, he runs the risk of deceiving himself, of seeking himself under the guise of seeking God—and of finding only himself, not God.

If you are attached to the exercises for their own sake, you are deceiving yourself; but if you regularly omit them, I greatly fear that you are presumptuous, unless you are simply letting yourself do anything you like. We are so made that we act a certain way, continue until it is a habit, and then justify our conduct by a theory concocted for the occasion. It is the easiest thing in the world to create a theology of oneself and one's whims. But this "theology" of whims, of the easy way, fills me with dread, when what we are looking for is a form of missionary life. There are always *rationes*

117

convenientiae and high principles which, when decked out in the latest phrases, will cover a multitude of things. We do not believe the reader will accuse us of being inclined to conformism. We have fought hard enough against the tendency to rely on methods just because they are old, as well as against shams and cheap contrivances of every kind, to have the right to voice our alarm when we see others throwing overboard restraints and ascetical practices and spiritual exercises under the impression that they are following out our ideas.

Since we are in the active ministry, and not in the seminary, you will allow me to make an appeal to you on behalf of souls. If you throw yourself recklessly into activity (even though it is highly spiritual and apostolic) and make no place in your life for sacrifice and for concentrated periods of meditation, your work will lose its vitality and it is souls that will be the first to suffer. You will, no doubt, use the same words as true missionaries; you will speak as well, perhaps even better; and your acts will possess the same external reverence. But there will be undertones and indefinable qualities missing along with the lack of a true interior life. And without these you will not ring true.

Let us take an example from the experience of all of us, whether we are young or already well advanced in years. Let us recall the period after a fervent retreat or after a meditation which was better made than usual; surely we can remember what our visits to the sick were like then, and our advice in the confessional, our words in spiritual direction, and even our welcoming smile in the sacristy. Now let us compare this with our behavior in similar situations a long time after the retreat or when we were spiritually at a low ebb. What should we conclude? Certainly that we must never allow ourselves to be taken in by the fact that from time to time—when we were least deserving, and from the most unexpected sources—things have happened to us which, like wonderful actual graces, served to give us the shock we needed. We must not count on having them happen all during our lives.

Let us be reconciled to the fact that we have to take the long, dark, and hard purgative way, with all the restraints and exercises that it entails. Afterwards, and only afterwards, will we be able to find God in the activities of our ministry. But "afterwards" is inexact, for we have no intention of defining a chronological order. First of all, we have no choice. We are in the apostolic life and it is in it and along with it that we must conduct ourselves in our search for God. Moreover, God gives Himself gradually, according to His good pleasure. And, above all, we shall never know whether or not we have arrived at that "afterwards": it is always possible to deceive ourselves. Never, and at fifty no more than at twenty-five, is a man definitively established in total union with God; self-distrust and self-denial, therefore, will always be necessary, and at no time will it be possible to dispense with the ordinary means to that union.

Let us go further, even though some who are anxious to be rid of all restraints may think we are overdoing it, and say that the nature of the modern apostolate itself requires us to keep a stricter watch over our interior life than ever before. To be closer to those we wish to reach, we want to be with them wherever they are, wherever they live and act; we want to be with them in their neighborhood and in their recreations, and even at times to share their life at work. We are not content to remain tucked away in our sacristy or rectory, nor to be the prisoners of a priestly routine on the pretext that any other course is dangerous. We refuse to change our course merely because it may be dangerous, and we are right. But, still, we must see that it is dangerous; we must not be blind to the fact that the atmosphere of the secular life into which we intend to go as priests does represent a threat to us and might end by "naturalizing" us. When we set out on these paths under the orders and supervision of the hierarchy, it is clear that the graces of our state will not be wanting to us if we ourselves are faithful. Some priests, however, have a very keen desire to join in this or that form of recreation, to dress as laymen even when there is little reason for it, and to adopt the standards of laymen. Is not this eagerness the manifestation of an unconscious naturalism? Even when it is under obedience that we are to try some bold experiment, this is but an added reason for bringing to it the most intense interior life possible. We recall hearing young seminarians describing the period they had spent in a factory. Some told us how easy it was for them to remain united with God all during a day of manual work in the midst of noisy machines and the humming activity of an industrial plant. "True enough," some of the older priests said to them, "but look out. You are still alive to the need to fill the void you find in this completely material life, and this is a new and startling experience for you. But wait until you get used to it. Then you will be no time in finding that the material and materializing life is threatening to invade you through every pore of your skin, unless you take pains to counteract it by a stronger interior life and to provide yourself with the support of an intense team life."

We want to avoid artificial occasions of meeting our people and to capitalize on all the natural occasions of doing so, and this is all to the good. But we have to be careful not to delude ourselves with words, not to give such a high-sounding word as "contacts" to what are only idle conversations, nor to speak of giving spiritual direction to families when we are satisfied with being invited to a meal or with passing a pleasant evening in a home.

It is a good thing to wish for an increasingly "spiritual" apostolate and to give it the preference over work which does not properly belong to the priestly ministry. But in that case we need to be highly spiritual men. Unless we are, we will no longer be accomplishing anything at all, neither the material tasks we have abandoned nor the spiritual work for which we find ourselves unqualified.

It is true that some predecessors of ours have fallen into a bourgeois existence, have succumbed to an official routine or settled down into an easygoing life. But at the same time let us not forget that in them this was the result of tendencies which are inherent in human weakness and are a threat to us too. If a priest turns into a bourgeois or a mere official, or if he becomes indolent, it is not methods which are at fault, but the way he uses the methods. The same natural inclinations can lead us into the same aberrations, even though our starting point and our ambitions are so opposed to them. It hurts us, for example, to find in our parishes many a venerable activity and many a confraternity no longer in line with today's mentality, just as it hurts us to see some of our fellow priests limiting themselves to a few of the faithful and faithfully tended sheep. But, on the other hand, it is not altogether uncommon to see a priest of another type doing much the same thing. He considers himself to be at the opposite pole from these last representatives of an outmoded spirituality, yet he himself gives all his time and solicitude and affection to some little conventicle of leaders whom he is visiting and cultivating all the year long. He streaks out ahead, as we mentioned previously, with a few souls who are more gifted or more capable of understanding him, and he forgets all about the rest. He does not suspect that he is succumbing to the very same temptation as his elder brothers, but for him, too, happiness consists in having a small circle of devoted disciples. It requires self-denial, and a great deal of it, to keep ourselves from acquiring a taste for such spiritual desserts and to preserve our appetite for more substantial and less delicate food. We can never dispense with self-distrust.

Some Materials for a Missionary Spirituality

In a word, we think it impossible for a priest to maintain his spiritual tone unless he finds a place in his life for meditation (to which we shall return later), for spiritual reading, for contact with the Scriptures, and for a real visit with Our Lord in the Blessed Sacrament during the afternoon. Only when he has the stimulus of such a preparation will he be able to celebrate his Mass with due fervor. We fear that even his breviary will become a burdensome routine unless the priest very frequently goes back over what he has read and gives himself the time to meditate on it.

Apart from the element of formalism, we believe that the traditional exercises do not sin by excess, but by defect. We can also understand why so many priests doubt their effectiveness. In the first place, there has been too much insistence on these exercises being kept up at any cost, and too little effort put into teaching priests how to live these exercises in the concrete circumstances of their ministry. Nothing harms a priestly life more than a formalistic fidelity to exercises which sets a man's conscience at rest without stirring it to life. In the second place, these exercises have been taken over unchanged from the monastic or seminary life and may be ill-suited to an active life. They need adjustments, and their shortcomings must be filled by something else. We shall have more to say on this later when we speak of the sabbatical rest and, later still, the spiritual life of the team.

It is very difficult to keep up the traditional exercises in a priestly life, and some of them ought to be completely revised; but, in addition to this, it is absolutely essential to realize that many priests neglect these exercises as not providing the needed sustenance and support. Until we take steps to enable the priest to receive support from the very framework of his life, his spiritual exercises will prove inefficacious most of the time. That is why we refer the reader to the sections which treat of the periods of renewal and the pooling of the team's spiritual resources.

MEDITATION

What must we do to be in continual union with God? What is the secret of being able to find God everywhere and always, without deceiving ourselves? How can we manage to be constantly charged with a true spiritual dynamism? There is, as far as we know, only one answer: arranging our lives so that there will habitually be room for what we have called intense or concentrated periods of meditation.

Many words have been expended on the question of "diffused" meditation or prayer. At the risk of perpetrating a bad pun, we cannot resist saying that we should be on guard lest our prayer be only "confused," while we are ready to consider it "infused."

We have, of course, no intention of proposing a method of prayer. In fact, we are quite convinced that the prayer which is best for us is the one which is personal to us, the one we have discovered after much groping and many failures and new starts. To us it would seem a mistake to consider the time given to prayer as a debt to be paid to God, a debt we could consider paid after we had put in the prescribed number of minutes or quarter hours. There is no such thing as a time of prayer after which we are free to go about our business with our minds at rest because we know we have taken care of our praying. No, it is the whole day which ought to be a time of prayer, and the vision of God ought to color everything we do. What we customarily call meditation is simply an exercise whose function it is to turn us Godward and enable us to see our whole day in a divine perspective. But it must, we repeat, be an intense period, intense enough to make its influence felt throughout the day.

And so we believe it is indispensable to set aside, every day, a short period of recollection and silence. This will be an opportunity for our minds and hearts to recuperate their strength, to take their bearings, and to open up to the grace of a greater intimacy with God.

When are we to make our meditation? It is quite hard to say. The first thing in the morning is the natural time for it; but we must take into account the weariness which remains from the previous evening, the drowsiness we feel when we have not had enough sleep, and the need of being in readiness near our confessional. To spend a half hour in church doing nothing does not mean we have made our meditation, for we cannot subscribe to that definition which makes meditation a half hour during which you do nothing else. In this matter, above all, we must determine to be realistic and to have no traffic with soothing illusions. Let us not be afraid to admit that there are periods when, for mornings on end, our minds are so lazy that we finally fall into a half-dreaming state which is simply a prolongation of the slumber nature insists on having. If we need to—no matter how old we are—let us have the courage to pick up a book, and, if this does no good, to take our breviary and recite it conscientiously. It sometimes requires more courage to force ourselves to say our Office well than to let ourselves fall into a prayer of quiet which has nothing in common with the peace of the soul lost in its Lord.

Why not postpone this period of concentrated prayer to a time when we will be better disposed for it—say, later in the morning or even the middle of the day? We at Colombes have found the period from noon until twelve-thirty a very good time for the whole team to meditate. We can easily prepare our meditation in the morning if we fail to do so the night before, and this midday meditation puts a stop to our activities and enables us to renew our strength.

What we are to do during this time will be sure to vary with temperaments and the graces God gives to individuals. We must not, however, forget that ours is an active life, this being a fact which our prayer should not fail to take into consideration. Unfortunately, it is a fact which often affects our meditation in ways we do not like. How can we be recollected when the problems of the previous evening are still passing through our heads, when we realize that we will have to spend the entire day trying to solve yesterday's unfinished problem or to undo yesterday's mistake? But is it so essential that our minds be completely free from such things? If our life is constantly overwhelming us with distractions, why should we not use these distractions as the subject of our meditation?

Let us suppose, for example, that we received a crushing blow last evening, causing us such shock and anxiety that we could not close our eyes the whole night long. In such a case, a very strong-willed individual may succeed in imposing interior silence on himself, but for a great many this is impossible. They should look at this wretched affair with God's eyes and speak to our Lord about it, asking Him for His light and, in their nearness to Him, finding the strength to face their problem. There is a story about a priest who made his meditation by taking up his agenda every morning and going over in God's presence everything he was planning to do that day. There is obviously a danger, and no slight one, of getting out of the atmosphere of prayer altogether; but, with a little good will, it is better for us to try to incorporate the troubles of the day into our prayer than just to put up with them, since it is likely that our minds will drift to them anyway.

On the other hand, there will be many days when our preoccupations will not be so absorbing and our minds will be free to seek solid nourishment. Have we not the Gospels? Will the time ever come when we shall have exhausted them? Meditating on the inspired text, we sometimes go too rapidly and devour a whole paragraph or a whole page, when a single sentence would give us enough nourishment for the day. There are days when we cannot get anything out of our reading and are unable to make a meditation out of it; but we must not minimize God's part. We may have nothing to say to Him and may be unable to find anything by ourselves, but surely He has something to say to us. Why not ask the Holy Spirit what special message He has placed for us in a verse or passage of Scripture? Only to a very slight extent is meditation a reasoning process: primarily, it is prayer, and the prayer of abandonment is the most valuable prayer of all.

Have we the good sense to force ourselves to do spiritual reading so as to provide nourishment for our meditation? We purposely say "spiritual" rather than "intellectual," for we are thinking of the kind of reading which nourishes the heart as well as the mind. The very act of reading is in itself an excellent stepping stone to meditation, because it introduces into our active lives a time of calm, a time of concentration of our interior faculties—provided, of course, that our reading is not limited to worldly or purely intellectual matters.

Then we have our Mass with all the riches of the Missal texts, and our breviary with the inexhaustible treasures of the Psalms! It is perhaps in these that we can most easily find suitable subjects of meditation, for the meditation themes in them are already clothed in the form of prayer. Taking our subject of meditation from them has the added advantage of helping to unify our whole life of prayer and of enabling us to celebrate our Mass and recite our Office more fervently.

One more thing. We must not hide the fact that

fidelity to meditation in our pastoral ministry requires a severe discipline of the will. But let us state just as emphatically that it will be even harder for us to say that our lives are a continual prayer if, in fact, we begin by capitulating when it is only a few necessary acts of the will that are required of us. If we find it impossible to impose on ourselves the brief period of silence which would enable us to find God, how can we possibly say we are able to find Him in the moments when we are very busy?

FAITH

If the priest is really to live the gospel and bring it to the modern world, it seems to us that he must really live the theological virtues of faith, hope, and charity.

In *Revolution in a City Parish* we stated that our people, especially working class people, no longer place any faith in logical argument. The best argument in the world leaves them unimpressed. But they are impressed by the man who speaks with conviction. The moment they can see a man is convinced of what he says, they show some sign of the respect and sympathy they feel. What they admire in him is nothing else but a faith that is really lived. We ourselves need the faith that made the Apostles say, "We cannot but speak." And the people need to feel this sense of urgency in us. It must shine through when we preach, for in no other way will we win the allegiance of the workers' world.

Let us not confuse this power of conviction with any special way of preaching. Even without a powerful voice or effective gestures a man can sound sincere. An individual may be thoroughly at home in the pulpit and quite unimpressive in private conversation. This is not faith. Faith shows itself as an interior fire which burns always and in all circumstances. Our Catholics, and even more our non-Catholics, should be able to discover that we really believe merely by observing us act.

A young man comes to arrange for his marriage. He begins by asking about fees and the difference between the various types of weddings. In reply the priest tells him that it is not the fee nor the kind of wedding that counts but his Christian preparation for marriage, and he adds a word to the effect that religion is not a matter of money. The young man replies at once: "In that case, Father, we can go right ahead; since you are doing this for us, I can see that you really believe in it."

How many priests are like that? They have the faith, of course. Péguy was exaggerating when, after stating what he believed in, he wrote to Lotte: "The maddening thing is that we can't trust priests. They have no faith at all, or very little. It is among the lay people that faith is still to be found." And yet, when we realize what was in his mind, can we say that he was entirely wrong? Is it not true, for example, that at Lourdes the fervor and courage of the people often put to shame the indifference of too many ecclesiastics? This blunt judgment of a young man can give us food for thought: "From the time of my first Communion I had nothing to do with the Church. Then someone gave me the Gospels to read, and I said to myself, 'This Jesus Christ is the real thing.

But priests, what are they? When they are the real thing and are more like Jesus Christ, then we will follow them. They leave you with such a strong feeling that they are only doing a job.' " Many sermons are given without conviction, so indifferently that they remind you of a lesson being repeated. We cannot but be uneasy when we consider the impressions Jacques Rivière confided to Claudel: "Do not believe that I have not tried at all. This morning I went to Mass. I tried to get hold of myself and pray. The Our Father is almost the only thing I remember now. I said it over and over again, but without succeeding in becoming attentive and without any fervor. I was not able to visualize God as being present. There are so many things you have to try not to see! Why does the priest confine himself to reciting the Mass instead of consummating the sacrifice? He was going so fast that he sputtered."

A real faith, the kind of faith that testifies to a personal experience of Jesus Christ, would produce very different results.

The missionary believes in the gospel, believes in it with his whole heart and soul. To him it is really a message of good news. To him the Sermon on the Mount is the only true map of happiness.

The missionary lacks confidence in indirect methods of reaching souls, and prefers the direct apostolate and the immediate contact which allows him to speak to men of God. He prefers it because he believes in supernatural methods and the attractiveness of Jesus Christ when He is presented as He really is.

It is in his own contact with Christ that he himself finds the light which shows him the way and fills him with joy. When, therefore, he goes to bring Christ to others, he goes with the certainty that he has the greatest possible riches and the finest possible present to offer them. He is so happy and proud to bear such a message that he does not feel any need to apologize for his insistence. And his happiness is more contagious and effective than a skillfully conducted discussion.

Since he believes in the transcendence of Christianity, hostile systems do not disturb him, nor does he feel it necessary either to refute them by argument or to offer sensational and provocative counterattractions. Not that he is afraid of a fight. The idea simply does not interest him: to believe in fighting means to believe in its methods; and he believes only in Christ's methods, which are to state the truth and present the message. There is an intrinsic power in the truth and the message which makes its own way into souls.

"He really believes that it happened." Precisely. He believes in the Incarnation, in Christ the Redeemer, in the Resurrection; he believes that God, and the man who is God's instrument, can do what is impossible to mere man. People may smile at him, but in the end he makes an indelible impression on them and succeeds in conveying his own convictions to those whom he meets. Pascal said he found it easy to believe in the stories of witnesses who laid down their lives to prove their truth. All men are like Pascal. They find it easy to believe in the man of faith, who is himself convinced of the reality

132

of the invisible world. They find it easy to believe in the missionary whose words and deeds prove that he is a witness of Jesus Christ. Is there a single one of us who has never been entrusted with the secret of the tremendous impression made on another by the radiating conviction of such a man? [1]

It is this spirit of faith which attracts others. It is the only thing that will enable us to speak out of the abundance of the heart. It will express itself in ways that we may find hard to define, but these are precisely the ways which prove convincing.

Is it not this very spirit of faith which will keep us from becoming functionaries and routine administrators?

Again, to have a profound faith means to believe in the attractive power of our religion in itself. Many men of faith have, of course, devised indirect methods of the apostolate, means that we shall presently call ersatz. Apostles whom we all admire have not hesitated to use external pleasures and worldly attractions as bait to gather around them a crowd of people to whom they might preach the gospel. But if we are to imitate them, eventually we must really preach the gospel to the people.

Besides, the reason we try dressing up the gospel in all kinds of human frills is all too often that we do not

---

[1] In Douai there are some religious who are workers. Two delegates of the C. G. T. (the Communist National Labor Union) were exchanging their impressions of them one day. "Have you talked with them?" one asked his companion. And he (the secretary of the Union) replied, "My friend, you don't have to talk with those fellows; you see the way they live, and that is enough."

believe that souls are hungry and thirsty for Christ and the gospel as such. We do not believe in the drawing power of our religion and the need of faith which is innate in the souls of men. Why do we not believe in these things? Because our spirit of faith is not what it should be and because we ourselves do not live sufficiently in the perspective of our faith. Why has a convert no hesitation about telling people of his discoveries? Because he himself is intensely alive to them, because he appreciates all the light which the faith has brought him, and because he is sure it holds the secret of happiness for others too. It is a lack of confidence in the magnetic power of our faith itself which makes us use sports and outings to attract the young. The same lack of confidence leads us to invent a whole array of external activities to enable us to keep in touch with families. We are convinced that no one will come to us unless he is brought by some material interest.

It is, on the contrary, the opinion of the author that our priestly lives are far too short to answer the needs of the men who are thirsting for nothing but truth and prayer and charity. If we do not hear them crying out to us, it is because our own faith is not strong enough. If they do not find in us the answer to their anxiety, it is because there is not enough conviction in our gospel preaching and in the very sound of our voice.

In the midst of the attacks made on our Church and our beliefs today, why do we so often assume the attitude of a victim or of a whipped dog? Is it not because we ourselves are not quite sure that our faith must triumph despite all this chaos, amid all this chaos, and even by means of this chaos? *Haec est victoria, fides nostra.* We are not sure enough of success. Some give up in discouragement after a timid effort—often the very ones who are at the same time busy on a personal spiritual system in which failure represents the ideal.

The missionary is prejudiced in favor of his brother priests. Because they have the same priestly character as himself, are animated by the same apostolic ambitions, and share with him the same priestly grace of Christ, he is inclined to judge their undertakings favorably even before he sees them in operation. Some individuals are always on the lookout for reasons to justify their suspicions and their condemnations, but the missionary finds things to admire and encourage everywhere. The suspicious critic has, in reality, but little faith; and, once he gets beyond the region of mechanical fidelity to a few formulas and traditions, he feels himself lost, and the Church with him. He takes his own theology for dogma, his rubrics for the liturgy, and his personal system for the Church. He has faith, but more in his own intellectual theories than in revelation or the gospel of Jesus Christ.

The man with real faith believes that Christ is always living in the Church. He believes that our Catholic treasures, the *nova et vetera*, contain inexhaustible riches. He believes that one and the same tradition has (according to the needs of the time) given birth to, carried along for a time, and then abandoned a great number of intellectual expressions, none of which was for a single

135

moment synonymous with tradition. Of course, there can be no question of denying that the hierarchy must keep a very close watch over the orthodoxy of all those who preach or act or write. We want only to express a decided preference for an attitude of fraternal under-standing over one of suspicion and criticism among priests who are fighting in the same cause, because the very Faith which all unanimously profess is on the side of the former attitude.[2]

---

[2] Cf. Cardinal Suhard, *Growth or Decline*, pp. 49–52: "We must not confuse integrity of doctrine with the preservation of its passing forms of expression . . . Undoubtedly we must scrupulously main-tain the defined dogmatic formulas. But must we identify revelation with theological systems and schools? [The Church has made the doctrine of St. Thomas her official teaching.] Must we conclude that St. Thomas has said everything, and that his thought has exhausted and equaled the revealed deposit? Must we now stop thinking? Obviously not. As Lacordaire expressed it: 'St. Thomas is a beacon, not a terminal.' His light should clarify an ever increasing investi-gation of the two sources of faith: Scripture and tradition . . . Tradition is by no means simply the mechanical transmission of an inert 'thing.' Rather it is the living communication and the pro-gressive manifestation—under the infallible control of the Magis-terium—of a global truth of which each age discovers a new aspect. . . . The same holds true for the discipline and the action of the Church in the moral order and in institutions. Should we identify tradition, which is life, with routine, which is death? . . . To preserve life, modernism sacrificed forms; to preserve forms, inte-gralism sacrifices life . . . Excessive traditionalism forgets one of the factors of the problem, and thus ends up in the same contradiction as modernism. While the latter made a norm of every value of today, the former makes of yesterday's forms the ideal of the present. This is a serious mistake of which Catholics should be doubly careful, first because this negative attitude of distrust of legitimate changes hampers the forward march of the Church, delays its penetration of the world, and risks furnishing pretexts for inaction to the average faithful; but especially because this habit of suspicion, if it assumes

Some Materials for a Missionary Spirituality

We must not let ourselves imagine that the faith of our brother priests is in danger the moment they seek to establish contact with the ideas of unbelievers. We must have enough confidence in their faith to admit that they can enter into discussions with unbelievers and mix with them, neither making concessions nor endangering the vigor of their own belief. If our faith is strong enough to surpass the convictions of men who lack the true light, why should not the faith of these priests be strong enough to do so?

If we have a deep faith, we will also have the missionary optimism which springs from it and which enables us to detect the action of the Spirit in our lay Catholics—for the Spirit is very often at work in them, even in the roughest of them. Since it is in this "multiform" Spirit that we put our faith and not in ourselves, and since we have St. Paul's admonition to "test every spirit and hold fast to what is good" (1 Thess. 5:21), we will be on the alert for the directions of the Spirit wherever they are to be detected, even when at first they are only stammered out. The bruised reed can become strong

---

a systematic form, would not be Christian. It would add a subtle danger of private interpretation to a lack of intellectual charity. For is not anticipating the hierarchy in its judgments, or even criticizing it for the initiatives it authorizes, a transfer of competence of which the least one can say is that it is not in order? Certainly it is not to this defensive retreat that the Church calls the faithful. Supremely exacting in all that concerns orthodoxy, ready for every sacrifice when it is a question of what comes from God and the apostolic tradition, she does not forget, however, the spirit which animates her interiorly. 'Extinguish not the spirit,' says St. Paul, 'but prove all things; hold fast that which is good.' "

again, and the wick with still a spark may once more burst into flame. We have no illusions: we know only too well how feeble the faith of many is. But, at the same time, we believe in the power of Him who gives light to whom He wills; we will not agree to "sacrifice" anyone, to permit anyone entrusted to us to perish.

The virtue of faith in the missionary of Jesus Christ manifests its presence by the need he feels to communicate his faith to others.

We must cultivate the virtue of hope too. Quite obviously, the missionary spirit is based on it. Almost as obviously, the reason why many lack the courage to undertake missionary work, or lose heart once they have begun, is because the virtue of hope is not there to give them courage.

Since childhood we have been reciting our act of hope. "O my God, I firmly hope that through the merits of Jesus Christ You will give me Your grace in this world. . . ." What is that "grace in this world"? It is the grace to assist us in working out our personal salvation, and we believe in it. But do we not also expect to receive the grace to assist us in doing God's work in this world and in bringing salvation to those entrusted to us? Do we not believe that God is more interested in our efforts than we are, and that it is always God who takes the initiative? How, then, do we ever manage to become cynical? "My dear young man," a pastor said to his assistant fresh from the seminary and full of enthusiasm, "you will get over it. In four or five years you will have lost your illusions. . . ." Was it not rather the pastor who had the illusions? For the assistant was full of the virtue of hope and, therefore, an integral realist. St. Paul said, "I can do all things in him who strengthens me." Should we not say the same? The grace of Christ is all-powerful, and with Christ's grace I am all-powerful too. The love of God can overcome the most recalcitrant of men and rouse the dullest of them; and I am the instrument of this love. Christ died for all; hence there are unlimited possibilities everywhere.

God is the prime mover in everything we do; still, that does not mean that He does everything without us, nor that hope can justify our indolence. Hope is not a passive virtue. It goads us into activity. It makes many demands on us. It is based on the Cross. Since we can do nothing without the Cross, we cannot be satisfied with setting it up by the roadside: we have to carry it. It is through the Cross and under the Cross, in spite of our falls and our failures, by getting up again after our falls and by making good our failures, that we do the work we have to do. Missionary hope is essentially hope in the Cross. We need only to go back over the story of our own apostolate to prove it, to be able to see in dim outline, behind the failures and the crosses, the redeemed souls we thought we were pursuing in vain. After a setback we will feel all the more energy to get to work— that is, to take a fresh approach to the work entrusted to us—for we will know by experience that the Cross is in it.

To believe that God is acting in us and through us is

to believe in Providence and to be sure that God will never abandon us, even in purely material matters. The chapter in *Revolution in a City Parish* which seems to have created the greatest stir is the one on money. It has earned us protests of every sort.[3] "But where are we to

---

[3] A few remarks on the question of money in our two parishes of the Sacred Heart and SS. Peter and Paul at Colombes may be in order here. We would like to point out that we have no secret source of revenue to call upon, and that we have to fulfill obligations at least as great as other parishes in regard to the diocesan funds. The reader must keep in mind that there are two types of parishes in Paris: parishes whose priests are in part supported by diocesan funds, and self-sustaining parishes (those which support their priests without outside aid). Sacred Heart parish belongs to the first class, SS. Peter and Paul to the second. This has enabled us to try out our system of eliminating fees and providing solemn ceremonies for all without charge in both types of parishes. At SS. Peter and Paul, however, we still receive something for funerals: we give the same solemn ceremonies to all, but those families which pay the undertaking establishments often make the offering which corresponds to the undertaker's class which they choose (though the offering made never goes beyond that for the sixth class). When we undertook to eliminate the system of classes at Sacred Heart, we made an agreement with the diocesan authorities whereby we would never ask the Chancery Office for an increase in our annual allowance, which was at that time 60,000 francs. Since then, the other parishes have had their allowance increased and now receive the additional amount required for the upkeep of their clergy. Sacred Heart parish alone continues to receive the same allowance, although there has been a continual devaluation of our money. In the case of SS. Peter and Paul, when we decided to abolish fees altogether, we made an agreement to continue the same contribution to diocesan funds for weddings, which was established by taking the average contribution of the preceding years. Our average contribution per wedding corresponded to the sixth class, and so for each wedding celebrated in our church we contribute to the diocesan funds the amount that it would have a right to from a wedding of the sixth class. Thus we have contributed the following amounts to the diocesan funds in the years 1947–1949:

	Diocesan Coll.	Church Tax	Deductions from Stole Fees
1947 (with fees)	71,576 francs	75,639	79,364
1948 (without fees)	134,230	133,558	120,874
1949 (without fees)	256,199	156,623	140,242

The increase in our Church Tax has been greater than these figures show. The actual amount of our 1948 Church Tax was 330,000, but the archdiocese established a ratio on the basis of the contribution of the parish in 1938, and the parish was allowed to retain the surplus. Our total income from collections has increased at the same time that we have been reducing their number. The Church Tax used to be taken up every month. At present we mention it only once a year, and the first year it went up 400%. This year, 1949, the increase continues, the total being 460,000 francs. The other collections, which are not prescribed and from which nothing goes to the diocese, show a similar increase. In 1948 these brought in 414,788 francs; in 1949, 504,014 francs. The reader may wish some information as to our means of support. 1. We have no list of benefactors and no benefactors from outside the parish. 2. We hold no bazaars or charity sales. 3. There is some assistance at Sacred Heart from the sale of publications, but this brings in much less than a bazaar or a charity sale. 4. In our first year we published nothing and had no income from royalties. All we have done is acquaint our parishioners with the financial situation and ask them to assist us directly rather than indirectly through a charity sale. They responded to our appeal. We should add that in each of our communities the number of priests and clerics is considerably in excess of the number of assistants for whom the diocese grants an allowance. Sacred Heart has one seminarian; SS. Peter and Paul has one seminarian and two deacons. Thus it is evident that our obligations are heavy. Where does the income we need come from? We can only say that Providence is evidently working through the normal sources of the revenue of a parish, the Sunday collection and the box in which the people may, if they choose, place offerings for the ceremonies which are provided without fee. Our books are open to any of our brother priests who desire more information. We are very anxious, however, that all should know the deep impression made by our change in policy. Even those who have least contact with the parish have been impressed. It has been a subject of conversation in every factory and place where men work, and it is still being talked about. It has won get the money to support the priests, our various activities, our parishes? . . . It is madness to give up assured revenues." But this is to forget there is a Providence. This is to forget that Providence will not fail to see that we and our parishes are supported, should it prove necessary or advantageous for the good of souls to suppress compulsory fees. Would this be the first time we lived on help sent us by Providence? We must not be Pharisees. If we can preach so eloquently on abandonment to Providence, let us at least have the courage to practice what we preach.

A young mother already has three children. When the last one was born, her already precarious health became further endangered. The doctor assures her that another pregnancy may prove fatal. Her pastor, when she tells him about it, advises her to trust in God's Providence, and with great courage she accepts the idea of the risk. But in another conversation with the pastor, the subject of abolishing classes and eliminating fees for ceremonies happens to come up. "That is a fine thing," she says. "It should be that way everywhere." "True enough," the pastor answers, "but it is a somewhat Utopian idea. After all, a man has to live." The woman, when she was telling us this incident, remarked, "What do you think of that? My pastor preaches to me on abandonment to Providence when it means risking my

---

the unfailing sympathy of the people for the clergy of the parish. We could quote hundreds of facts and proofs. If it were necessary, we would go down on our knees and beg our fellow priests to consider the idea of abolishing fees.

life, and he is not willing to run a much slighter risk for God's work."

We must be careful not to let any plan for increasing our apostolic effectiveness serve as a pretext for placing our hope in anything but God. It is in God, and not in human means, that we must hope. People deceive themselves when they trust in things which they consider a source of strength, but which in reality are unsteady and unreliable. They hope in God, of course; but in the final analysis they are eager to have the backing of political power, the security money gives, the favor of powerful friends, the prestige of a well-turned phrase, and the strength that derives from solidly established activities.

When they have to get along without these advantages in which they have put their faith, they are upset, afraid of the future, desperately determined to recover them. Yet none of these advantages can do anything to convert a soul, to lay the foundation for God's work, or to produce the slightest movement of love. Something has gone wrong with their hope, for the Christian virtue of hope should have the opposite effect: making us appreciate the insecurity of everything which is of this world. The time for us to start feeling uneasy is when all the worldly signs are favorable to us and we enjoy the protection of the powerful and the financial support of the rich. *Deposuit potentes de sede et exaltavit humiles.* "The *foolishness* of God is wiser than men and the weakness of God stronger than men" (1 Cor. 1:25).

It is hope that enables us to take our place alongside

the mass of common people. For what is the great drama of the workingman's life, and the ever-present source of anguish in the workingman's home? The insecurity which is always with him. Our people are at the mercy of the slightest incident or accident: a prolonged illness, a crippling injury, a strike, a period of unemployment— and the whole family is in want. At the beginning of the year there is never any assurance that the children will not be going hungry by the end of it. A workingman's life may begin in comfort and end in destitution. But with us priests it is different. There are some of us who have never known what insecurity is, and we have too little experience of real privation. We are always saying that we have chosen the better part. We should not forget that these words, as Our Lord used them, had reference to contemplation and attachment to God alone, and no reference at all to the anxious concerns of Martha. I am not forgetting the destitution of many priests in the country, but it is not these who refuse to abolish fees (which in their case constitute a very small part of their meager income). Why are others, who have never done without anything, so averse to abandoning themselves to God's Providence? If we were to accept the same insecurity as our people, would it not bring us closer to them in their suffering?

Let us continue with our act of hope. "My God, I await with a firm confidence . . . eternal glory with You in the other life." Without doubt, it is the next world which counts, and people often reproach us for thinking only of Paradise and forgetting this life. We know the familiar slogan about religion being the opium of the people. But there is another side to the picture. All our efforts to reach a better world really enable us to establish contact with the aspirations of all our people, for they too are searching, uncertainly and in the darkness, for what is to come, for a new world.

If the missionary whose work lies in the workers' world is complacent or resigned, he has no chance at all of understanding that world or of being accepted by it. He will find it easy enough to win a hearing from people who are complacent in their lives and ways, but he will not succeed in killing their complacency, and thus will do no good to them. The workers' world is anything but complacent. It is in constant movement. There may be alternating crises of hope and despair, but through them all there runs an obstinate and unchanging aspiration for a great change to take place and a new world to arise at long last. It is all too easy to laugh it off and say, "Of course, they long for the day when all the poor will be bourgeois; and, when that day comes, their desires will be satisfied." It is true enough that many of them want only a life a little less tormented or a little more comfortable. Would anyone think of blaming them for that? But the man who really knows the workers' world realizes that there is more than this in their aspirations. Even when they are not personally its victims, injustice revolts the workers more than other people. They are haunted by the dream of a state in which all will be brothers. When anyone speaks to them of justice and brotherhood, and on a world-wide scale, he is always sure of moving them.

There is little, if anything, in this world of ours that is perfectly pure; and these aspirations of the workers are, of course, sometimes tainted with materialism. But if we cannot see that these longings represent hope in an obscure form and constitute a good soil for Christian hope, then we do not know our business. These people are yearning for a better world. What is it our mission to announce, if not this? What did Christ come to bring us, if not this? "We announce to you a great joy: a Savior is born to us." "And there will be new heavens and a new earth." We have no idea of indulging in double talk: it is not our mission to announce an ideal economic system, a "Christian" technique of social life or happiness here on this earth. Just as we do not dream of restoring medieval Christendom considered as the supreme ideal of the organization of nations under papal direction, so we have no idea of establishing a social system in which everyone would be happy because society would be in conformity with the gospel. We know that such a temporal triumph of the gospel—which in itself would be the ideal, since it would surely stamp out war and injustice—will always be thwarted by the selfishness of men. We also know that Christ never promised it to us.

Yet we do hope in and announce "the kingdom of God." What does this mean? To all Christ's followers it means, in the first place, the City of God in heaven, where there will be no more tears or suffering, but only

146

unending joy in love. Yes, it is heaven we hope in—and so much the worse for unbelievers who scoff and speak about opium of the people. Our conscience bears us witness that we are not preaching resignation to injustice when we say that injustice will one day be vanquished and that those who have believed in love will know happiness, whereas all oppressors will suffer eternal defeat. We know that with the same words we are preaching both the interior kingdom and the happiness on earth which is the experience of all who consent to carry their cross and follow Christ. We preach the Beatitudes promised to the children of God, and at the same time we believe that it is the peacemakers, the meek, those who hunger and thirst after justice, and the pure of heart who will be at once the happiest of men and the architects of happiness for others, even in suffering and opposition. Finally, we proclaim as a doctrine, as the teaching of the Gospels and St. Paul and the Popes, respect for every human person, the solidarity of all men as the creatures of the same God and the brothers of the same Christ, the precedence of brotherly love and the common good over individual interests.

A social evolution, contained in germ in the message of Christ, has slowly come about under the influence of this teaching. No historian would deny the pre-eminent importance of Christianity in humanity's forward march toward a more just and human social order. Lacordaire spoke of it as "the progress of humanity under the light of the Cross." It has gone on in spite of opposition and even of temporary relapses; for there are obstacles to this progress and deviations which reverse the trend for a time, but they are all derived from doctrines or movements opposed to the gospel. We are therefore justified in hoping that the more there is of the spirit of the gospel in the world, the more firmly the "kingdom of God" is established in the souls of Catholics; and the more fervent Catholics there are, so much the more will this earthly city of men reap good results, even temporal ones. Since we are animated by such a hope, there is no reason why we should not plant it in the workers' world whose evangelization is in our hands; indeed there is every reason why we should. This workers' world has been fooled by false prophets a thousand times, and yet it is still hoping that tomorrow will be better than today. It is simply unthinkable that we should meet such a world with an attitude of scoffing scepticism or with a pseudo-supernatural indifference. Perhaps the future holds no better living conditions for them; but justice and love are ours to give them, and these are never called into play without leading to a better life for men. A missionary, if he is alive to the legitimate longings for the better life which fill the world, will make them his own and include the people's hopes in his hope.

It is our duty to announce the gospel, that is, "the good news." We have retained the word "gospel," though it almost seems as if we had agreed that it is no longer to mean "the good news." Listen to catechists and preachers, and see whether or not you feel that they have news to announce—or whether they have not that tone of voice which warns you their news is sad rather than good? Are our parishes and our Sunday congregations "good news"? You would describe them better as stale or out-of-date or stereotyped news. It all seems so dull and dreary, as if you had seen and heard it a thousand times before.

To show the ambassadors of John the Baptist that He was really the Messias, Jesus pointed to this proof: "Tell what you have seen: The lame walk, the deaf hear, the dumb speak and the poor have the gospel preached to them." Could we say the same of our parishes? We would be more likely to say: "The people who come here cannot hear any more; they cannot speak any more; they are completely paralyzed. And as for the poor having the gospel preached to them, alas! alas!"

What is it we need to make us missionaries? What is it our little group of Catholics needs? It is this virtue, this tiny little virtue of hope, as Péguy would call it—a virtue which ought to make us at once poor and confident, and give us the power to have the song of the "good news" always on our lips.

CHARITY

We could, taking charity as a starting point, cover all the pastoral problems with which a missionary has to deal. And we can say without exaggeration that it is impossible to imagine a missionary without charity. The missionary mentality is, in fact, the result of the stimulus provided by the twofold commandment: "Thou shalt love God with thy whole heart, and thy neighbor as thyself." These two commandments are similar—a fact we never see more clearly than when we analyze the missionary mind, which is the child of the first commandment as well as of the second. Some plunge into the missionary life because they cannot bear to see God's love disregarded; others, because they cannot bear to see their brothers in darkness.

The missionary must foster this charity, which will make him expendable at all times. It would be true to say that, if his heart is filled with charity, the other virtues will be given him as well; but true only if his charity is the real thing—that is, love. Priests speak of charity being a virtue, but some of them would perhaps hesitate to speak of love being a virtue. Our ecclesiastical language should not make us forget our native tongue. This is not a mere matter of words; like other words, these are signs of realities. In the efforts to give us a spirituality at the seminary, it is hardly love which receives the greatest notice. And when love is mentioned, we are left with the impression that it is something quite distinct from—love! We are not told often enough that we are loved, that we have been chosen through love, that the choice which singled us out (*Ego elegi vos*) is an entirely gratuitous act of predilection, of which love alone is the source. We are not told often enough that we have been chosen to love, that it is our mission to love, that a priest without love makes no sense. We are not told often enough that it is just as illusory to love God without *really* loving the people in our care as it is to pretend having a priestly love for men

with no love for God. We cannot exercise the priesthood in its fullness unless we love those whom Jesus
loves and unless we have a burning zeal for the welfare
of those to whom we are sent.

It is strange that this zeal could appear to be lacking
in a priest: that people could be with him and not sense
a heart full of love and solicitude, but find him cold,
distant, heartless and rarely moved by anything but
administrative difficulties or theoretical discussions. Yet
this phenomenon exists, and much more frequently than
it should. Parishioners can live in a parish for twenty
years and never see a priest come into their home or the
home of any other workingman. A young worker, only
sixteen, can go to Mass every Sunday for more than a
year and never be contacted by the priest in charge of
the Jocists. Important high schools and large public
elementary schools can have assigned to them as chap-
lains priests who are unable to do the work. A sermon
can be a frigid instruction or a piece of unctuous non-
sense without a breath of life in it. Ninety per cent of
the people in a parish can stay away from church, and
the talk and the preoccupations of the rectory be entirely
unaffected by it. Are these not signs which indicate that
zeal is not the dominant virtue of some priests?

And yet Jesus has chosen us. It is His will that His
love should reach certain of His sheep through us. He
has given us His heart in order to love them. It is in us
that some men must find what Christ came to bring
them—above all else, His burning charity. Had we His
look, the look with which He regarded the people at the

151

multiplication of the loaves, "and seeing these people, he was moved with compassion for them because they were harassed and exhausted like sheep without a shepherd," would we not be moved with compassion too? There are the sheep condemned to die of hunger because they do not know where the pastures are, nor the road leading to them. There are the sheep born for the immense riches of Christ, and not even knowing that Christ exists. There are the little ones, the weaklings, looking anywhere for nourishment, looking even to deceivers for it, and letting themselves be imposed upon and exploited. And they are all sheep that belong to Jesus personally. He is there in the midst of them, but they do not know it. It is on us that He is counting; we might say that He is counting on us alone to show them this, to enable them to see Him looking at them with real affection. Unless He reaches them through us, they will not be reached at all. This is a tremendous responsibility. If we looked at them with His eyes, could we be listless and indifferent? Could we act toward His people as did the Apostles before Pentecost, calling down fire from heaven on the towns that would not receive them, or keeping people away from Jesus lest their loud appeals annoy Him? Or could we re-enact the priest and the levite passing by the wounded man of Jericho as quickly as they could? It is now the period after Pentecost. We too have received the Holy Spirit, the "sacred fire." What are we doing with that fire? It ought to send us out of our cenacle, just as it sent the Apostles out of theirs. Our habits constitute our cenacle; so does our narrow-mindedness and the fine company that surrounds us, for none of these has anything to do with love. If we have the fire, it ought to make us spontaneously prefer looking after the "sheep without a shepherd." When the missionary is animated by the charity of Christ, he identifies himself with Christ, as Christ intended and still intends him to do, and to such an extent that he loves the sheep as if they were his own. Yet the same reason prevents him from seeking to keep them for himself and helps him efface himself in order to bring them into contact with their only Shepherd. He feels a real need of going out to others, and to those who have the least. It is a need that gives him no rest: *irrequietum cor.*

We must understand that the people of today's world have no more belief in love than they have in God. They believe in selfishness, in every-man-for-himself, in the instincts of self-preservation and self-defense. Our poor people see themselves trapped in a jungle from which there is no escape. It is the law of the jungle which holds sway, with everyone snatching as much as he can from the claws of the rest. When we show our people that we love them—that we really love them, individually and unselfishly—we have already given them their first taste of revelation. If we are to reveal to them the existence of a God who is Love, the first step is to love them in His name in order to let them discover that they are loved by us. Especially with people who are so thoroughly materialistic to begin with, no Platonic love will do it, but only a charity that is effective and that makes itself felt in practical life. Only this charity will show us that in our parish there are people poorly housed and undernourished, suffering people of every kind; only this charity will let us see every case, not as a case to be filed away in our records, but as a personal case on which we are going to work with all our heart until we have seen it through.

It should now be clear what we mean by "charity." It is a fire stronger than anything, the same fire that Christ came to start on earth. It is the very thing which characterizes the heart of God. We have received the heart of God, the very love He has for men, the love which carried Him even to the sacrifice of the Cross. "There is no greater love than to give your life for those you love." This love ought to make us desire the good of those we love—and every sort of good, temporal as well as supernatural. This, and nothing else, is apostolic charity. This is also the missionary spirit. We are missionaries to the extent that we are "charity," as Christ Jesus was.

Those who mistrust the missionary movement as not interior enough, and those who depreciate it as "activistic," fail to understand that it is above all a movement from within, the same thing that St. Paul's life and letters are filled with: the *caritas Christi urget nos*. Like every other love—but more than any other love, because it is the greatest of all—the charity of Christ drives us ahead, spurs us on, insists, demands. But it demands not only that we run after the sheep, but also that we do whatever else this entails in the way of humility, self-denial, service, poverty, common life and, above all, union with God.

It is by such charity that the mission idea will take hold of us interiorly, will come to rule us, to dominate our every thought and moment and instinct, to take complete possession of us.

We may conclude that there is no better way for the missionary to cultivate the spirit of his mission in himself than to develop the three theological virtues. But this conclusion is no mere point in a seminarian's meditation. It contains the very foundation and the indispensable demands of the missionary life. If our seminaries are not sending forth as many apostolic souls as we would like and if our clergy retreats fail to kindle the missionary flame in many priests, the reason is that these virtues are preached for their own sake, and not from the viewpoint of the mission life and the problems of the day.

A CARDINAL MISSIONARY VIRTUE: GRACIOUSNESS

In *Revolution in a City Parish* we attempted to show the importance of welcoming people, of meeting them with a smile, and of making all those who come to us feel at home. We also tried to show what a decisive influence the welcome which people receive in the sacristy may have on them. At Colombes we always speak of the priest "on welcome" rather than of the priest "on guard." [4] It is more than a mere matter of words. At any rate, we want to make it clear that this virtue of graciousness is not just a matter of external deportment or an art of treating well the parishioners who come to us; it is even more than a good means of reaching their souls; it is a virtue, and one that our priesthood itself requires of us.

Under a different name (possibly *amicitia* or *affabilitas*), St. Thomas would probably have classified it as one of the subdivisions of justice. Would he also have seen certain characteristics of charity in it, and perhaps some features borrowed from the intellectual virtues as well? At least, it is certainly not found under this name in the traditional classification. But we have made it plain that we are not writing a treatise on spirituality. In looking over missionary life, we discover that this ability to welcome people is something quite distinct from a method of the apostolate. We see it as a kind of supernatural instinct which opens the priest's heart and mind, renders him receptive and understanding, and makes him a door, a *porta coeli*, through which all human values can find their way to God. It is in this sense that we call it a virtue and, by analogy, a cardinal virtue, for it seems to us that it is one of the hinges of our priestly spirituality.

We would be glad to have a theologian help us when we look at God to see what basis there is in Him for

---

[4] These are literal translations of *"prêtre d'accueil"* and *"prêtre de garde."* The term *accueil* is the new virtue which is the subject of this section and which is here sometimes translated, for lack of a better word, "graciousness."

this virtue of graciousness. What is the Holy Trinity but one Person constantly welcoming the others? Might not God, as He stoops to His creature, be called the "One who welcomes"? He has brought creatures into being so that they might return to Him; He became flesh that they might have a way by which to return. He has placed in His creatures an appetite for Himself, to guide them in their gropings toward Him, the Supreme Good. In the Parable of the Prodigal Son He represented Himself as the One who waits, who receives, who holds His arms open. In the Gospels and in the Apocalypse He is the "One who returns," whom we are on our way to meet. He made man and therefore knows what is in man. He knows that every man is infinitely original, although all are created in the likeness of the only God. He knows that men do not come off a production line, but that each one is a unique phenomenon in the history of the world. And that is why there are many mansions in His household. He made us free and He respects our freedom; He treats us as friends to be invited, not as slaves to be forced.

These expressions of the divine psychology (St. Thomas would say the *mores divini*) and these comparisons which invite us to fathom God's mind, help us to see the attitude God's minister should have toward souls. The minister is not greater than his Master. He should not appropriate souls to himself, nor lord it over them. He is not to worry them or turn them away, but to welcome them with the same impulse of love which is at the origin of Creation and Redemption, the love which is expressed in the gospel destined to be announced "not only to you, but to all those who are afar off, even to all whom the Lord our God calls" (Acts 2:39).

It follows that a priest has to be gracious and friendly. But not only because this is a wise and prudent policy, such as a man might adopt if he failed to understand the true value of souls and yet had to respect them if he wanted to win them. No, it is love that imposes this graciousness on the missionary. God loves every soul. Every soul is infinite in value; and we ought to love every soul in spite of its wretchedness—and, indeed, even because of its wretchedness, since it was because the souls of men were so wretched that the Redeemer poured out His blood. The priest should often make his meditation on this point, keeping his whole flock before his mind or dwelling on one or two individuals whom he might be tempted to neglect or who seem to him less well disposed.

If every Christian ought to be a unifying influence, a "catalyzing agent," wherever he is, what are we to say of the priest? By the very fact that his is the priestly office he is a shepherd, a man of the flock, a man who belongs to all. He has been "ordained" for the salvation of his fellow men—that is, appointed to see that they are saved.

The word "pastor" makes no sense except in relation to a flock. The pastor must provide himself with a soul big enough to embrace all his flock. His heart must beat in unison with the flock. He must, for the sake of the flock, nourish himself that he may be able to nourish the flock. He must be able to feed himself by feeding them. It would not be going too far to say that the flock will be healthy only if he is healthy.

Let us take Sunday as an example. To every Christian, Sunday is the Lord's day, the day of the Resurrection, the day of joy. Now, for the pastor, the feast consists in being there in the midst of his flock, not in getting away from the flock to find a more recollected atmosphere. His Mass is his prayer. Whether he celebrates it himself or helps his people assist at it or is merely present at it in their midst, the Sunday Mass is his joy and the full flowering of his prayer. In our opinion, it is even quite right for him to forget his purely pastoral work on this day. Let him leave visits and catechism and societies for the rest of the week, and on Sunday renew his strength by permitting himself the joy of being with all his people. The idea of his isolating himself in his office, once he has said his Mass, on the pretext that there is nothing more for him to do in church, is altogether appalling. If he does this, his is not the Sunday of a true shepherd.

The shepherd ought to live with his whole parish. He has not the right to slice off a choice portion of it for himself.

The pastor, as we have already said, must beware of leaving the main body of troops behind as he streaks out ahead with an advance platoon; he must realize that it is only as a unit that the parish will be missionary.

The pastor must also be careful not to impose his own

brand of spirituality on the parish. This is a danger especially to the young missionary, to the one inclined to the esthetic and the esoteric, the snares of which we have already pointed out. Why must we avoid doing this? The reason is that the parish embraces all kinds of spiritualities and even many people who seem to have none at all. The reader will remember what we said in the third chapter about "old Catholics." We have to make allowances for the differences in souls, for their differences in temperament, and for the fact that some find it easier than others to follow a new lead and that some go ahead faster than others. There is the lady, for example, who is president of the Perpetual Rosary Society; even in a parish we might call evolved, she will be part of the existing reality and count for something. There is the group of graduates of the parish recreation center; even if it seems to be a nucleus of resistance to change, it is part of the parish and each of its members has a soul.

We have to think of such people, listen to them, and take their existence into account when there is question of the parish making some step forward; nor should we regret having to give them such attentions. It is not a waste of time for us now and then to try to take their pace. Sometimes this may be hard, humiliating and discouraging, but it is always a hardship for a young man to adjust his pace to that of the old man with whom he is walking. Is this not still another missionary mortification?

Being gracious will often mean knowing how to wait,

not being impatient to gather in a successful harvest, to register a conversion too soon, for example, or to bring a soul back to the sacraments before the time. "When grace does not come by the direct road, it comes by a roundabout way. When it does not come from the right, it comes from the left. When it does not spring up like a fountain, it may, if it chooses, come like the water which secretly oozes out under a dike on the Loire" (Péguy, *Clio*).

When an engaged couple comes to us and the young man is not baptized, it is being gracious to ask why he wants a religious marriage and, if he asks for baptism, to point out to him that there is no obligation for him to be baptized in order to be married in the Church. It is being gracious to set people free from an obligation which the Church herself does not impose. It is not uncommon for young people to come back later and ask us to prepare them for baptism or first Communion. "If you had insisted on this before marriage," they say, "I would have done it simply because you required it, but I would not have been sincere in the least. Now I am coming to you by my own free decision."

The Church, as Father Congar says, is a building which is constructed both from above and from below. How can it ever be built from below unless the priest graciously welcomes the observations and inspirations of the laity, of all the laity without exception?

Graciousness is not a passive virtue, but fundamentally an active one. From the standpoint of our actions, it means that we must not only welcome people when they

161

come to see us in our office, but that we must also go out after them. And likewise from the standpoint of our mentality: it is not enough to listen to people; we must also try to know them as well as possible, put ourselves in their place, live their life, share their sufferings, go to them in order to be with them—not to "catch" them. The reader will recall the scene in the movie *Monsieur Vincent* which shows St. Vincent in the presence of the Cardinal who wants to appoint him Chaplain General. St. Vincent answers him: "Leave me with my poor. I no longer know the face of a single poor man, the name of a single poor man." It is this personal knowledge of people that is the important thing.

Being gracious means knowing what the people who speak to us can do and what they cannot be expected to do, and taking this into account. As we become more experienced in the direction of souls, a serious danger threatens us: the danger of believing we have seen everything, and so of acting by analogy and of placing the person we are dealing with in a category we have already met. People sense this, and it hurts them. It is not possible to classify human beings and personal dramas in this way. The life of every individual, and every period of it, is a drama which is his alone. Every individual is a creation and he has no duplicate.

For the man who has a general responsibility, for the pastor especially, there is still another danger. He is all taken up with the broad aspects of his charge and the general interests of the parish, and is therefore inclined to neglect individual cases, to treat them as negligible quantities, and to consider those who seek his help as so much business to be got through with. But unless this graciousness of ours enables us to enter sympathetically into individual cases, what good is it?

To be the pastor and guide of souls is a wonderful calling, and by appreciating our role we will avoid these dangers. Our role is not to dictate the policy to be followed, as we would have it, but to conform ourselves to the will of the Holy Spirit. It is to listen, to discover, to aid each soul and the whole parish to follow the inspirations of the Holy Spirit. We must not get in the way of the Spirit. "The Holy Spirit," as Father Varillon expresses it figuratively, "does not generally blow in the pipes that are prepared for Him in advance." We must believe that; our experience will often bear it out.

And thus our virtue of graciousness is not limited to the gracious welcome we give to souls; it is even more important to give a gracious welcome to God.

A Prayer of the Abbé Godin

For all the brothers and sisters and little children, for all
    those sons and daughters of Yours
That You have entrusted to me, O Lord, with their
    lovely and noble souls,
And for the knowledge of You that I owe to them,
I thank You, O Lord, and I praise You.

For all the souls redeemed by Your blood, O Christ,
    who have come into my life,

To whom I failed to give the message You gave me for
them,
I ask Your pardon, O Jesus.

For all the men and women You put in my path,
Whom I abandoned, because I was indifferent or too
busy,
Like a bad shepherd who does not know his sheep,
Have pity on me.

And for the good seed which You once sowed,
Which grew up slowly,
And which will go on growing to the end of the world,
Every day I pray to You, O Lord Jesus.

For all the men and women the Lord Your Son has given
me,
With a prayer and a plea I turn to You, O Worker
blessed among women, nurse of all souls, Light of
all mornings,
O Our Lady!

AN EXERCISE TO ADD: THE SABBATICAL REST

Perhaps there are too many exercises in the list
presented us in the seminary—we are not competent to
say. But at any rate we are proposing still another
exercise, which we call *the sabbatical rest*.

In Genesis we are told how God obliged men to rest
one day out of every seven. There is no reason to think
priests are exempt. There may be priests who waste their

time. But there are certainly many others who would be happy if they could have, not an eight-hour day, but simply an eight-hour night. We think that for them it is necessary and even indispensable to rest one day in the week. Certain priests, for having entirely lost sight of this fact, now find themselves handicapped by bad health as well as by weakened morale.

It is worth while observing that in general we think too much in terms of the day and the rhythm of the day. Modern life is measured rather by the week than by the day. In regard to the workingman, for example, we no longer speak of an eight-hour day, but of a forty- or forty-eight-hour week. In regard to the priest too, although we often forgot it, life with all its complications and variations spreads out over the whole week. The priest's daily schedule no longer allows him to get adequate rest: often there is no such thing as the evening period of relaxation; the night's rest is curtailed; the day's intellectual work is disturbed; and the morning meditation is frequently broken into. The priest must therefore see to it that he gets a *weekly* period for physical rest, intellectual work, and meditation; nor is this so difficult as it might appear at first sight.

To be more specific: there has been, as we mentioned earlier, a great deal of discussion concerning the value and opportuneness of the spiritual exercises in the traditional sense. Some have indicted them on the charge of having been transplanted from life in the monastery to life in the world, deeming this enough to condemn them. Some have accused them of being too burdensome, incapable of fitting into our modern life. We observed, however, that these practices sinned by defect rather than by excess, and by that we meant precisely that the exercises of the sabbatical rest needed to be added to these daily exercises. The daily exercises may be all that the monk or the scholar needs, because the monk or scholar can go directly to study or to the recitation of the Office or to meditation with a mind at rest. He lives at all times in an atmosphere of peace and intellectual life. Our lives, however, are full of agitation, and we go to prayer or study with our heads crammed with worldly or even apostolic concerns. We have just finished attending to two or three matters, and we know that our presence will soon be required elsewhere. Thus, the few moments we have managed to save, with great effort, for renewing our interior life are as full of agitation as the rest of the day, and it is sometimes easier for us to count the times we have been without distractions than to count our distractions themselves. But since this is not so in the weeks following our annual retreat, it is clear that what we need is, not time, but rather a soul attuned to study and meditation.

If so, why should we not take one whole day of rest every week? Let us get away from the parish altogether beginning Sunday evening—and I say Sunday *evening* intentionally, because the night is as important as the day. Let us take refuge in a religious house where we will not hear the rectory doorbell or the voice of our good housekeeper, and where we will not know whether or not someone is asking for us. Before Monday evening comes, we will be able to give ourselves the rest our system needs and to renew ourselves intellectually and spiritually. We have hardly any idea what such a day of relaxation can mean to a man who is wholly absorbed in the active life, or how much *time* there is in a day—time in which to get things done, not time to "kill." It is incredible how much a man can accomplish between morning and evening when he is left in peace.

This weekly exercise seems to us the most important of all, and we hope that seminary rectors and spiritual directors of priests will do their best to see that priests make it part of their schedule. If all the other commandments of Genesis do no more than codify the natural law, whereas this one alone is a positive precept, may it not be because this precept comes closer to being a natural law than we had imagined?

On this day of rest, after a good night's sleep, we will be able to spend two solid hours in meditation and reading; we will have the joy of reciting our Office in peace, and will still have plenty of time to plan our week and outline the following Sunday's sermon. On this day we will write whatever we may have to get ready: articles, conferences, reports. We will set out for home again with peace in our souls, our minds alert once more; and our work the rest of the week will be ten times more effective, thanks to the sabbatical day.

If we pastors allow ourselves this day of rest, clearly we must allow it to our assistants too. We think it is not enough to allow them to have it: in many cases we shall have to insist upon it. There is no reason why in larger parishes we should not draw up a regular schedule of sabbatical rest for the priests. The faithful will very soon learn that Father N. is not in on a certain day of the week, but they will understand also that their priests take the time to think over the problems entrusted to them.

Several months ago at Colombes the question arose among ourselves whether some of us at least should not go to work in factories. To be as certain as possible that we would make no mistake, we asked several of our finest lay militants what they thought of the idea. Most of them favored the principle of our going to work; but one felt differently and explained his view as follows: "We laymen are wholly taken up with the preoccupations of material life, and we have not enough time either to pray or to think. So we want to work hard and contribute our money to enable you priests to think and pray for us, to allow you to be free from work and material worries in order that you may study and give us the benefit of your studies." This man was not far wrong in the way he envisaged our life, nor would he think we were failing in our duty if we allowed ourselves a day a week for the purpose of renewing ourselves spiritually and intellectually.

A sabbatical rest every week. Do we not also need a *sabbatical week* at least once a year? We do not mean a week's vacation. Vacations, if they involve travelling (no matter how beneficial it may be), often leave us exhausted. Nor do we mean the priests' retreat, which is of course indispensable. What we mean is a week devoted to reviewing the year that is past and to preparing for the year to come. It would be good for us, with all our assistants or with the priests of the deanery, to take a week in which to relax together and study the main directions of our parish apostolate. Nothing as stiff and formal as a meeting or a session behind closed doors, but rather a week of relaxation in common. At the end of it we should be closer in hearts and minds: an atmosphere of joy is always a great help when there is serious work to do.

We believe in the sabbatical week, and even more strongly in *the sabbatical year*. Life is continually sapping our strength, and in the ministry it is all too easy to lose our intellectual habits. Moreover, one generation is not the same as the next, and the great intellectual interests change, while we are fighting at close quarters with pressing difficulties. Now and then we wake up to the fact, always a surprise to us, that we no longer understand the young people and that they no longer understand us. It would be good if this happened to us more often. It proves that we need to take our bearings carefully again and apply ourselves once more to some serious study.

How are we to do this? The Jesuit Fathers have their "third year," during which they return, in principle at least, to the scholasticate, after having been some time in the ministry. The Mission of France is thinking of making it possible for its members to have a "third year." Why could we not allow ourselves a sabbatical year three or four times in our lives—every ten years, for example. Perhaps we could arrange for it before assuming a new post. For such a year there would be need of a house suited to the purpose, with a good library, a superior who understood his role, and a rule—but a rule framed for priests who have been engaged in the ministry. All the residents of this house would be there by their free choice. Perhaps it would not be easy to obtain such a house; but it would be worth the trouble even if only ten or twelve priests experienced in apostolic work came there every year, priests who could pool their experiences and make them available for scholarly research and who would have a chance to prepare themselves for a new stage in their lives.

Finally, we shall have to read the first chapter of Genesis once more. After six days, when He had finished His work, God rested. There is in that a hint for us from God, a hint that we too should stop when we have done all we can do. This means: a day will come when we ought to realize that all the good which can be expected of us has already been drawn out of us, that it is time to retire and leave the field to others. To have the sense to retire in time, to give in one's resignation in time, is to observe another law of nature. Alas! how many fail to do so. Let us have the good sense to give ourselves this rest, our last rest on earth. Let us do so in order to prepare ourselves for the day of the Lord, but also as a charity to our brothers and as a sacrifice for the common good of the faithful. We will serve them best by handing them over to others.

VI

The Absolute Need of Teamwork

IN *Revolution in a City Parish* WE DEVOTED A GOOD DEAL of space to the idea of teamwork. It might therefore seem unnecessary to reiterate our strong belief in the advantages the team offers us or to expound once more the functioning and the details of team life.

But the years have passed, and time enables us to test many things. It leaves some institutions crumbling or covered with ashes, others more solid. Some ideas develop; some acquire depth. In our earlier book we advanced many ideas on various subjects, but we can say unhesitatingly that it is the idea of the team which has struck the deepest roots in us and done the most to prove itself. At that time, we suggested quite a number of new directions, but team living now seems to have proved itself the best by far. Indeed we have never once questioned its value. More and more we are coming to look upon it as fundamental to missionary life. The longer we are in the ministry, the more it seems that every time we run up against a difficulty or have to solve a problem, the team always and without fail holds out possibilities which, had we been isolated, would have been out of the question. Whenever we have had occasion to envisage the general problems of the apostolate in France, and even outside of France, and to admit its shortcomings, we have at the same time had the feeling that there was only one remedy: team living. Whether it is a question of the control we have to keep over ourselves or others, of striking out in new directions, or of assuring continuity in our work, the answer is always the same: see to it that there is a team. Nothing will slip past its collective vigilance; its judgment guarantees greater security; its permanence will protect our work from being disconnected and disrupted.

It is probably an incurable weakness of humanity to look for easy methods and ingenious contrivances. We often have priest visitors who expect us to supply them with such appliances for their apostolic work. At times they tell us in detail about their difficulties and the impossible situations they are in. We always reach the same conclusion: it would be easy to solve the difficulties if there were a team.

For us, therefore, it is no longer a question of simply putting forward the idea of the team. We did that four years ago somewhat timidly, for one is always timid when one speaks of something for the first time. We can now state the conclusion we have come to with the passing of the years. It is this: there is no substitute for team living and teamwork; nor are these merely an indispensable means of getting much more work done and making it much easier for the priest to develop his spiritual life; they are indispensable almost by a natural necessity, like a biological entity inherent in the authentic life of our priesthood and pastoral ministry.

THE THEOLOGICAL BASIS

We presume permission to make two statements, the one based on theology, the other on history, even though we have no intention of writing a tract on theology or history to substantiate them. The first is that the priesthood is not something personal to each one of us, but is inconceivable except as a participation in the priesthood of the bishop. The second is that the "presbyterium" was originally a team participating in the priesthood of the bishop and giving expression to it by its activity.

To be more concrete: when several priests are working in one parish, it is absolutely necessary for the faithful to have a clear idea of the unity of their priesthood. It must be made possible for them to abstract from the individual priests and to see their priesthood as one thing —one thing in space and in time. But we all know only too well that such is not the case. In how many parishes is it a reality? Rather, everyone singles out one priest as the center of influence and credits all the success to him. "I am for Paul, I am for Apollo." It is not a new phenomenon. The very first contribution a genuine priestly team makes to a parish is to show the people that it is useless to try to monopolize Father X or to make a hero out of Father Y. Fathers X and Y will not stand for it, nor will the other members of the team.

The Missionary Spirit in Parish Life

The people of the parish must learn one lesson so well that it becomes an instinctive reaction: they have at their service, not several priests, but a team. This does not, of course, mean that the priests will not have their special tasks, nor that a person who wishes to consult the priest of his choice on a matter of conscience will be denied his right to do so. But it does mean that no priest is going to be excessively monopolized.

On our arrival in our new parish of SS. Peter and Paul at Colombes, we chose the priesthood as the first subject to preach on. This we did to enable our Catholic people to see the purely spiritual role of the priest in its true light and to grasp the fact that the priesthood of the team was one priesthood. "We really feel," one of the girls said to us, "that it is a team which is at work in our parish; and we find it reassuring to know that, if one priest or another leaves us, we are not on that account going to be abandoned." And since then we find our parishioners themselves constantly speaking of the team. It is always: "Does the team agree on this?" "Has the team thought of that?" and so on.

That is what we meant by the unity of the priesthood in space. Unity in time is even more indispensable. We do not remain in our parishes forever, and very often the departure of a pastor or an assistant brings on a disaster; when he dies or moves on, it means the end of every activity which revolved around him, of everything he started or directed. But this can hardly happen when there is a team in the parish instead of individual priests working independently. The team lives on and, through it, the priesthood. There will perhaps be dark moments now and then, when a member of the team has to move and his personal qualities are missed, but this will never mean a complete disaster.

Here, from our own experience, is an example of this "perennial" nature of the priesthood. When half of the team, the pastor included, left Sacred Heart to go to Grand Colombes, there was no faltering because the pastor was leaving or because others were accompanying him. The parishioners were aware that the team was still there, and they said so.

On the other hand, we remember the pastor who was assigned to another parish and wrote, for the last issue of the parish bulletin before his departure, a message to this effect: "The following twenty-two projects I had decided to carry out in the parish. So far I have been able to translate only two of them into reality." His poor successor has his hands tied, and will be in danger of losing the respect of his parishioners unless he can manage to see eye to eye with his predecessor on all twenty-two points!

THE ADVANTAGES FOR US PRIESTS

For us priests the team has this essential advantage: it helps us realize that it is our priesthood which counts, not our person. The team obliges us, if we may use the figure, to pass our priesthood through a filter and rid it of every element not proper to it.

In connection with our spiritual exercises, we spoke of the great danger there is of their being omitted or losing their value unless we have the reciprocal control and example which the team gives us. We must explain ourselves more fully here. We are becoming more convinced every day that the spiritual exercises cannot have the effect they should have apart from the favorable atmosphere the team provides. Our team life has flowered since the first five years at Petit Colombes. There was, to begin with, a community of action and thought, and this has brought us quite naturally to a greater community of soul. Every member of the team—or of both teams, as we shall say hereafter—is now much more aware of what is taking place in the souls of his brother priests. All have taken responsibility for each of the members. When there is a falling off in fervor, or an increase, it is common to all. When we meet now, it is no longer merely to plan our work or to pray. It is quite common for members of the team to confide their spiritual difficulties to one another or to pool their spiritual resources. There is a perpetual exchange among us, and a constant reciprocal enrichment. In addition to the parish council meeting at which we study the problems of the ministry, we also hold a weekly meeting concerned with the spiritual life at which every member of the team acquaints the other members with his actual spiritual condition. Sometimes we discuss a subject previously agreed upon, and each man strives to make the greatest contribution he can. Sometimes, when one member is more qualified for a particular question, he gives the rest of us the benefit of his study and experience. It is obvious that such a meeting is worlds removed from those sessions in which one man holds the floor throughout, and the rest have only to listen—for the fact that a man is the superior of a house does not necessarily mean that he is qualified to preach the gospel to the rest. In our meetings everyone has something to say; to be more precise, the Holy Spirit is given an opportunity to speak to all through the particular graces given to the individuals. In this way, a common soul is forged and we come to feel the solidarity of the team.

This seems the right place to answer a question which a number of priests have put to us. Some confreres of ours, whose good intentions are obvious, ask us if it would not be right to begin by pooling the *spiritual resources* of a group in this way. It is true enough that the team which at the beginning planned to restrict the team's activities to mere *work* done in common would be in a very insecure condition. But it is impossible to divide a living thing in that way. Both things are necessary, and provision must be made for both. Yet we cannot disregard the laws of life. We should begin by living together, and the first thing we should ask ourselves to accept is the mortification of team life. Later on, and almost naturally, the "spiritual life" of the team will strike deeper roots. Some priests think that the members of a priestly team spend their time in mutual contemplation of one another. This is not so. The life of team members is like the life of friends: it does not consist of stopping to look at one another, but in marching ahead together toward the same goal. And it is by our marching together, sometimes after having journeyed the whole day, that the evening brings us an experience like that of the disciples at Emmaus: "Was not our heart burning within us while he was speaking to us on the road?"

The team helps us intensify our spiritual life. We are convinced that the team is also a great help in intellectual work. At the seminary we were told that we must not think our education was finished once we were in the ministry, but that we must continue our intellectual work. Almost the only means suggested was reading. But we must realize that many priests are so heavily burdened by their duties that they have little time to read. If many activities tend to dissipate the life of the soul, they have the same effect on the life of the mind. It will perhaps be said that a man has but to do himself a little violence and adhere to regular periods of reading if he really wants to further his education and continue developing his mind. This is obviously an excellent method of enriching the mind. But let us be honest with ourselves. Men of action are not to be treated as if they were scholars. It would be close to the truth, we think, to say that men of action keep up their intellectual life quite as much by listening and speaking as by reading. We have no time for extensive reading, and all the exhortations in the world are not going to change this situation in the least. Even if we did have time, there is no guarantee that extensive reading would necessarily raise our intellectual level. We know priests who spend long hours in their studies, who devour all the reviews and follow the latest developments even in the field of abstract thought, but who seem to do little more than passively take it all in. It provokes no reaction in them. The reason is that they lack the life that comes from the spoken word, and especially the ability to react that comes through exchanging ideas with others. For some priests who are isolated in their country rectories a personal intellectual life is out of the question, often because they can see no sense in storing up ideas and knowledge which they will never use, but more often because—with no opportunity to exchange or compare or discuss or refine their ideas—the ideas they derive from books come into them as exhibits into a museum.

It could be that the remedy lies in giving priests opportunities, not so much to read books, as to hear specialists who really have something to give them. One of the good points of the team is that it can invite to the common table men whose conversation is extremely rewarding. In the course of an hour's conversation an author will often give us the substance of his book; and later, when we have time to read its three hundred pages, we will derive much more profit from them because of the stimulus his presence gave to our minds. We can talk and discuss a subject with such a person; and, after he is gone, we team members can go on with the discussion. More often, we members can take turns reporting on our reading, putting it into the common stock for all to discuss; this is a great help and a precious timesaver.

In a word, though it is good to insist on our keeping up our spiritual and intellectual life, it is no less necessary to devise means of enabling us to do so. Those hitherto suggested fall short of the mark and most often prove failures. If we are to supplement them and make them effective, we need help. We believe that team life can help us as nothing else can.

We can already hear an objection: "But you just mentioned our brother priests in the country. Do you not think team life is out of the question for them? Are you not afraid that what you say will discourage them?" It is true that our experience has been mostly in the city, nor do we deny that it is much more difficult to start priestly teams in the country than in the city. Yet Canon Boulard, in his *Missionary Problems of Rural France*,[1] pointed to a number of priestly communities and teams which were already functioning in rural districts. We ourselves know that there are such teams in almost every part of France; and we know also of a number of deaneries in which the priests, without living together and without ordinarily being able to work side by side, have found ways of meeting frequently and of forming a real work team.

We do not say it is necessary to live in community, but we do think it is absolutely necessary for the priests of the same deanery or the same region to pool the resources of their apostolic, intellectual and spiritual life,

---

[1] *Problèmes missionnaires de la France rurale.* The reader of this English translation may be interested in knowing that in many respects this book parallels *Revolution in a City Parish*, although the factors that are responsible for the decline of Catholicism in the countryside are somewhat different from those to which it is usual to trace the loss of faith among the working classes in the cities.

which cannot possibly be kept up to the mark with the minimum of meetings the deanery conferences represent. Though the team is obviously not a universal remedy for all the weaknesses of the missionary movement, it is an indispensable factor in missionary work. The very existence of such a little community of thought and prayer and work will overcome many of our defects, many of our troubles and failures.

As we go on living this team life and seeing what it enables us to accomplish in our parishes, we are constantly meeting evidence which proves that such team life is almost a physical necessity.

We aim to make our parishes real communities. But the more closely we examine the missionary problem, the clearer it becomes that we cannot make converts (especially in a workers' milieu) unless there is a community for them to join, no matter how small. Our parishes have to become communities with some warmth about them, and the warmth must radiate. We believe that parishes cannot achieve this transformation unless they have at the center a priestly nucleus to animate them. There is a comparison which seems to fit the subject exactly. Our parishes are like the cells of an organism, which, if they are to live, must have a vital nucleus at the center. Without such a nucleus, they consume themselves; they live on their reserves for a time, then they waste away. They continue in existence, but in an existence without life. It has been our lot to hear the grievances of many priests, both pastors and assistants. They have told us they were helpless to do

181

anything to revitalize their parishes in view of the resistance either of parishioners who form a block to protect the stagnation with which they are satisfied or of their fellow priests who refuse to move at all. Now, these priests lack neither zeal nor intelligence nor energy. Their only fault is that they are alone, with no one to share in their plans and their actions. What do they need? They need that sense of vastly increased strength which the combined efforts of several priests would give them; they also need to feel that there is one will animating the actions of several men; but even more they need something which it is impossible to define exactly in words or even in thought. We may perhaps be satisfied with calling it the radiating influence of a small community on a larger one, and it is like the power of a living thing to create new life.

We might find it useful to continue the analogy in the matter of multiplying teams.

When we are called upon to infect a parish with the missionary fever, the task ahead of us is not easy. To undertake this work, which requires exceptional prudence and initiative, we have to form many teams; and, in making them at once bold enough and reliable, we have to suffer many a headache. There is the problem of choosing the captain and the members of the teams, whether these are chosen by the members of the team or associated with it by authority. Once the team is established, there is the difficulty the members have in getting to know one another and in agreeing on principles and their application. All this takes time, and the time consumed in the clash of temperaments and ideas may test our patience to the limit. But the worst is yet to come, for it still remains to be seen how the parish will react to the decisions the team makes. The parish's reactions are of the greatest importance and value, but we must know how to interpret them correctly and distinguish superficial resistance from serious opposition. Priests of different background and mentality, if they have only recently been formed into a team, do not find it easy to draw the same conclusions from the reaction in the parish. They may all be willing enough to undertake a certain new work; but if they go about it timidly, because it is new to them all, the project may come to grief at the first obstacle it meets. This would not happen if there were at the center of the group several members who had already carried through such an undertaking elsewhere and were able to give the team the benefit of their experience.

We are sure to encounter all these difficulties if, when we seek to form new teams, we insist on sending into the parish where missionary work is to be started priests who are new to teamwork and to one another. Whether it is a new pastor in the midst of old assistants or a whole team composed of new elements, the result will be the same. It is like sowing seeds. Such priests will require time to learn the parish and to decide on the steps they must take. They can easily fall a prey to doubts. There will be the doubts, for example, of each individual concerning his own ability or the ability of the others, doubts on the meaning of the parish's reactions, doubts concerning the team's power to survive. There will be much indecision, many discussions, and also—if we are willing to face the facts—many failures. We know only too many of these experiments which died almost as soon as they were initiated. Yet they began with the best intentions and all the good will in the world.

Are such fumbling and uncertain methods inevitable? Would it not be possible to avoid them by propagating new teams from existing ones? Obviously, what we are suggesting here is not the only possible method. For a long time to come, it will be necessary to start teams with members, all of whom are new to the life. A start has to be made. But surely, the moment it becomes feasible, the solution we propose is more in accord with the laws of life and better adapted to the special difficulties of the modern apostolate. We are not proposing it as an untested theory. It is the fruit of the experiment we tried when we divided the team at Sacred Heart in order to take over SS. Peter and Paul. Part of the team went to Grand Colombes with the author, and the rest stayed on at Petit Colombes under the direction of a former assistant who became the new pastor. Both teams were brought up to the required number by aggregating new priests to them.

When the Cardinal Archbishop of Paris asked us to take this second parish, he did so with the idea of enabling us to apply the same missionary methods to a whole section of the city. There are many advantages in such combined work, but they were not immediately apparent. We have had to wait for both parishes to arrive at the same stage of development, and that stage has not yet been fully reached. Still, from the beginning we had one advantage on which we had not counted: we discovered that in the second parish we had the support of a team which had previously grown to maturity as a unit. At the heart of the new team there was a nucleus formed by years of living together and working together. From the outset we could see what a great source of strength this was: we were spared a great deal of groping and were able to see openings right away. There was no temptation to try experiments which had failed at Petit Colombes. This held true both for the community life and for the work of the parish. We had the immediate impression that, with no extra effort, we would be able to cover the same ground in half the time. We can truthfully say, for example, that we have done as much in two years to make the parish into a liturgical community as we accomplished in five years at Sacred Heart. It is obvious that, with so much work to be done on all sides, we are not making such rapid progress in other forms of apostolic work—getting to know our territory and our people or starting communities of lay people. And yet even in this field we have benefited, for we set to work at once on the basis of our previous experience, and up to now it seems quite clear that the parish has gone ahead more rapidly. The lay people have been much quicker to grasp their role. If there is a delay, the fault lies with us priests who have too much to do. The lay Catholics are not lagging behind, nor are they offering us any opposition.

Not that we should ever go into a parish like heavy-handed colonizers eager to apply ready-made methods and ingenious contrivances transplanted from other fields. But it is easy to see how great a help such a unit can be for the new members of the team and for the entire parish, for it is a real unit, whose members have the same ideals and ways of life, and between whom there is reciprocal trust. The parish sees and realizes that its priests are united by the life they lead and by their love for one another, and it is around this nucleus that the whole parish community will be formed. We repeat that this is not the only way teams can be multiplied. But might it not be more generally applied?

Only a large team can propagate itself in this way; a small team cannot afford to split off a group to provide a nucleus for a new team in another parish. But there is nothing to prevent us from putting in a parish twice the number of priests needed and leaving them there for four or five years, after which a division could be made for the purpose of taking over a new parish.

The number of priests this requires may cause some to protest vehemently: "How are we to do it, when we are so short of priests that we cannot even provide them for all our parishes?" We do not admit the justice of the protest. On the contrary, we think this system is the best answer to the present situation of the clergy and the parishes. Over and above the advantages of this system which we have already pointed out, there are others which might result from increasing the number of priests in certain parishes: 1) where there is real missionary work to be done, and 2) where there is a desire to provide young priests with a good school of apprenticeship.

Advantages for Missionary Work

The process of dechristianization is so far advanced that superficial remedies cannot really cope with it. You cannot cure tuberculosis with poultices or cough drops. Parish missions lasting three weeks or a month do produce good results; they have been, and they still are, effective when it is a question of stirring up parishes that are still Catholic. When there is a mission in such parishes, everyone is aware of it; and, as they all have the faith, it is enough to shake them out of their indifference and to lead "sinners" to conversion. But with our working class, posting up notices of the opening of the mission is not sufficient. The people will pay no attention. To our knowledge, several parish missions in Paris failed to attract as many people as the Sunday Masses. Even in such cases, of course, the mission serves to wake up the faithful Catholics and to make a few "conquests." But, if we really wish to accomplish some true mission work, we have to give time to it, as much as several years perhaps. Preaching is not enough. There is need for work at all levels. And the work will have no lasting effect until a Christian community has come into being and all the lay people have put their shoulders to the task, with the priests teaching them to understand their role and inspiring them to assume responsibility for the whole neighborhood.

187

The Missionary Spirit in Parish Life

It is obvious that even a few priests will accomplish something; but they will do so at a very high price and at the risk of losing their health, their spirit, and their enthusiasm.

Do we see what will inevitably happen if we let things go on the way they are going? It is reasonable enough to wish to provide every place with a priest, and we all shudder at the prospect of leaving any village without one. Nevertheless, we must face the facts, no matter how unpleasant they are. If we go on trying to fill all the needs, what will the outcome be? Priests will be overburdened and will be able only to look after the "dispatch of current business." In the rural areas especially is the situation critical. It is impossible for the priest even to provide Mass and teach catechism in all the districts for which he is responsible. Tired out from long trips by bicycle or motorcycle, his legs and feet aching, he is not in the right frame of mind to be able to welcome people smilingly or to give them the support they should have. What is worse, the priest burns himself out bodily and spiritually. His health succumbs to overwork, and he becomes disheartened. Have we not too often seen young priests full of spirit and with high ideals lose their enthusiasm and their buoyancy after a few years of such a life? Should we be surprised when we recall the crushing burdens they have been called upon to assume?

If these priests were living in a community, the situation would be very different; if there were a number of them together, they would be able to do something more than superficial work. They would have time to accomplish real missionary work, to make lasting contacts, and to engage in some genuine study. At the beginning of this book we mentioned the need of taking very special care of the "priestly instrument." If a kind of paralysis seems to creep over the lives of so many priests and they appear to be constantly losing their dynamism, where are we to put the blame? In part, perhaps, on their personal shortcomings, but much more on the conditions in which they have to live.

The bishops are fathers to us. They are understanding enough to see in this list of grievances nothing more than the plaint of one of their priest sons. The words come from a priest who has often seen his brothers break down and cry, and who now has the boldness to speak aloud—but with respect and love—of the suffering he has so often witnessed.

All of us tremble, and with good reason, at the thought of sending priests to work in factories or mines. It is certain that they will have to face many dangers. And yet they are on fire with apostolic zeal as they take up the work, and there is good reason to hope that the contrast between the materialism of the life they see and their own high ideals will give them a healthy shock. Furthermore, these priests generally form part of a community, for good care is taken to see that they are not left alone.

What do we think will happen to the young assistant who, after two or three years in the priesthood, is sent off to a deserted region far from any priest colleague and with almost no truly spiritual work? How is it that we do not fear much more for him than for the priest workman, since we have seen so many of the former lose heart or enthusiasm in such conditions—and sometimes much more than heart or enthusiasm?

The present state of affairs even causes loss of vocations to the priesthood. What he has before his eyes is what attracts a boy to the priesthood. Now, the sight of priests all taken up with business and material concerns is not one to fill a boy or a young man with a longing to do what he sees them doing. Let us suppose that an assistant is removed from a good parish and not replaced, because an abandoned region needs one more pastor. Who is the more likely to stimulate vocations—the young assistant who is full of enthusiasm or the pastor who is on in years and far too occupied with administration? Nor should we expect vocations from neglected parishes, but from Christian communities, where piety and the faith of parents and children provide the proper soil for these choice plants to thrive.

We ask pardon for these remarks. We could not speak thus were we not convinced that our present policy condemns us to move in a vicious circle, whose radius, unfortunately, is likely to become smaller and smaller.

The system we are suggesting does indeed require the sacrifice of whole areas, and this is painful to consider. Besides, the system does not promise immediate large-scale success. But when there is too much to do, is it not the rule to begin at one end and not try to do everything at once? When we try to do something everywhere, we end by doing nothing permanent anywhere.

The Absolute Need of Teamwork

A Good School for Apprentices

The forming of teams would offer priests, especially young priests, the advantage of an excellent school of apprenticeship.

We all realize the importance of the first years in the ministry. The seminaries are often blamed for failing to prepare seminarians adequately for the difficulties they are certain to meet. In some instances the criticism is undoubtedly justified. At the same time, almost all young priests, when they come out of the seminary, are full of generosity and zeal and the will to give themselves. How is it that after four or five years in the ministry far too many of them lose these qualities? It seems to us that we can explain it only by admitting that a young priest's very first contacts with pastoral life may get him off on the wrong foot. The influence of his first pastor and the example received from his older brothers are of primary importance in forming the mentality of the young assistant. There is great danger that his youthful enthusiasm may not prove strong enough to withstand the baneful effect of the sacristy slogans, the hasty statements, and the deanery conference criticisms to which he is subjected. When you take his surroundings into account, you come to believe that the result was inevitable.

We must also bear in mind that the first contacts with the ministry are often very trying. Unless the young priest is understood and enjoys the companionship not only of a good pastor but also of other priests hardly

191

older than himself, his first year is an intensely painful experience, as he lives through his dark days alone and solves his problems without knowing to whom to appeal for advice. The mere change from the regulated activity of the seminary to the liberty of being able to organize his personal activity tends to make him fritter away his days and at the same time be convinced that he is overwhelmed by his duties. We have seen young assistants killing themselves and bemoaning the fact that they were doing nothing, and we know how much they suffer. What better remedy could there be for this than to have parishes which could absorb young priests and gradually initiate them into the secrets of pastoral work, parishes in which they would find real missionary work to do instead of the wearisome round of parish societies and administrative tasks?

In other days there were "priest schools." Their accomplishments in the way of intellectual formation are perhaps questionable. At any rate, they were an excellent means of providing an initiation to pastoral life, for the candidates had opportunities to visit the sick, to receive people at the rectory, to teach catechism, to look after the church, and so on. At the present time no pastor could assume responsibility for such a "priest school," but there is no reason why a team might not become a school for apprentices.

And then there are the religious communities. Up to now they have furnished most of the missionaries for parish missions. Could they not now come to the aid of the secular clergy? Would this not be a modern way of giving a mission? As their contribution, the religious would offer their habits and traditions of community life, and the seculars would teach them how to make real contact with the masses. Nor is this a mere paper plan. It is already a reality in Marseilles, in Paris, and in Colombes, where religious from different Orders and secular priests trained in different seminaries are living a true community life and closely cooperating as a team in their work. If we mention the fact, it is, as usual, simply because we desire to make a contribution from our own experience in the hope that we may throw some additional light on our common problems.[2]

It is only our personal experiences that have given us the courage to write as we have written here. We are filled with embarrassment at the thought of it, for we have touched upon questions of policy which it belongs to the diocesan or religious authorities to formulate, and not to us. We beg them to pardon us for our audacity. "One has always," according to Father Doncoeur, "the right to weep before a father."

But we had little intention of weeping, and none at all of remonstrating with authority—for we realize only too well the impossible situations which our fathers, the bishops, have to cope with. And the affectionate respect we bear them enables us to suspect something of their suffering and solicitude in the face of problems for

---

[2] Useful information may be obtained from the team of priests which is now at work at Saint-Séverin (2, rue des Prêtres-Saint-Severin, Paris V*e*).

which it almost seems there is no solution.

Thus it is not to them we had any intention of speaking. Indeed, the Holy Spirit used Balaam's ass to point out to the prophet the way he was to go, but we do not think of ourselves as filling even that lowly role. Some priests have, however, seen fit to confide their difficulties to us, and we have to admit that the obstacle they encounter when they desire to undertake something or to start off in a new direction is sometimes the very wall of priestly opposition. How can priests be expected to form a team if they have not been trained with this in view, if they have never had any experience of this life or even any thought of it? How can we bring priests in undermanned parishes to accept the idea of a certain parish being given more priests than are actually required for the parish work?

It was because we had priests in mind that we felt it was our duty to let our ideas be known. The priests we have in mind are those of our brothers who are actually in the priesthood and the seminarians who will one day live that same life. It is for these, for these alone, that we have spoken. We must create a strong current of priestly opinion; we must change the outlook of priests; we must make the best use of all the resources at our command— for then, and only then, will it be possible for our fathers, the bishops, to make the decisions they judge opportune.

A NOTE ON THE TYPE

IN WHICH THIS BOOK IS SET

This book is set in Janson, a Linotype face, created from the early punches of Anton Janson who settled in Leipzig around 1670. This type is not an historic revival, but rather is a letter of fine ancestry, remodelled and brought up to date to satisfy present day taste. It carries a feeling of being quite compact and sturdy. It has good color and displays a pleasing proportion of ascenders and descenders as compared to the height of the lower case letters. The book was composed and printed by The York Composition Company of York, Pa., and bound by Moore and Company of Baltimore. The typography and design by Howard N. King.